Spiritual
Warfare

BY DR. DAVID JEREMIAH

Turning Point

Published by Walk Thru the Bible Ministries, Atlanta, Georgia.

Printed in the United States of America.

Contents

About
Dr. David Jeremiah
and Turning Point

D r. David Jeremiah is the founder of Turning Point, a ministry committed to providing Christians with sound Bible teaching relevant to today's changing times through radio broadcasts, audiocassette series, and books. Dr. Jeremiah's "common sense" teaching on such topics as family, stress, the New Age, and Biblical prophecy forms the foundation of Turning Point.

Dr. Jeremiah is the senior pastor of Shadow Mountain Community Church in El Cajon near San Diego, California, where he also serves as President of Christian Heritage College. He and his wife, Donna, have four children.

In 1982, Dr. Jeremiah wanted to bring the same solid teaching to San Diego television that he shared weekly with his congregation. Shortly thereafter, Turning Point expanded its ministry to radio. Dr. Jeremiah's inspiring messages are currently broadcast weekly from over 300 national and international radio stations.

Because Dr. Jeremiah desires to know his listening audience, he travels nationwide holding "A Night of Encouragement" radio rallies that touch the hearts and lives of many. According to Dr. Jeremiah, "At some point in time everyone reaches a turning point, and for every person that moment is unique, an experience to hold onto forever. There's so much changing in today's world, sometimes it's difficult to always choose the right path. Turning Point offers real people an understanding of God's Word, as well as the opportunity to make a difference in their lives."

Dr. Jeremiah has authored nine books including *Escape the Coming Night* (Revelation), *The Handwriting on the Wall* (Daniel), *Exposing the Myths of Parenthood*, *Turning Toward Joy* (Philippians), and *Turning Toward Integrity* (James).

About This Study Guide

The purpose of this Turning Point study guide is to reinforce Dr. David Jeremiah's dynamic, in-depth teaching on *Spiritual Warfare* and aid the reader in applying Biblical truth to his or her daily life. This study guide is designed to be used in conjunction with Dr. Jeremiah's *Spiritual Warfare* audiocassette series, but it may also be used by itself for personal or group Bible study.

Structure of the Lessons

Each lesson is based on one of the tapes in the *Spiritual Warfare* audiocassette series and focuses on a specific passage in the Bible. Each lesson is composed of the following elements:

• Outline

The outline at the beginning of the lesson gives a clear, concise picture of the passage being studied and provides a helpful framework for readers as they listen to Dr. Jeremiah's teaching.

• Overview

The overview summarizes Dr. Jeremiah's teaching on the passage being studied in the lesson. Readers should refer to the passage in their own Bibles as they study the overview.

• Application

This section contains a variety of questions designed to help readers dig deeper into the lesson and the Scriptures, and to apply the lesson to their daily lives. For Bible study groups or Sunday school classes, these questions will provide a springboard for group discussion and interaction.

• Did You Know?

This section presents a fun fact, historical note, or insight which adds a point of interest to the preceding lesson.

Using This Guide for Group Study

The lessons in this study guide are suitable for Sunday school classes, small group studies, elective Bible studies, or home Bible study groups. Each person in the group should have his or her own study guide.

When possible, the study guide should be used with the corresponding tape series. You may wish to assign the study guide as homework prior to the meeting of the group and then use the meeting time to listen to the tape and discuss the lesson.

For Continuing Study

A complete catalog of Dr. Jeremiah's materials for personal and group study is available through Turning Point. To obtain a catalog, additional study guides, or more information about Turning Point, call 1-800-947-1993 or write to: Turning Point, P.O. Box 3838, San Diego, CA 92163.

Dr. Jeremiah's "Turning Point" radio broadcast is currently heard on more than 300 national and international radio stations. Contact your local Christian radio station or Turning Point for program times in your area.

Spiritual Warfare

INTRODUCTION

On a Sunday evening in Russia a few years ago, believers were gathered secretly in a basement to worship the Lord. While they were singing a hymn, the door suddenly burst open, framing two armed soldiers. "Everyone not willing to die for their faith had better get out!" they screamed. Quietly, some of the people began filtering out. After a few moments, one of the the soldiers shouted, "This is your last chance! Turn against your faith in Christ or suffer the consequences." Only a faithful few remained, huddled together as one of the soldier shut the doors, locked them, and strode forward. "Raise your hands," the other said quietly, "but raise them in praise to God. We are Christians, too. We just wanted to know who we could trust."

Faced with that situation, what would you have done? Christians in America have never experienced the kind of persecution that goes on in other parts of the world, so perhaps they are not as aware of the fact that we are in a spiritual battle-zone. The Bible says that we are in a war; that we are wrestling against the powers and rulers of darkness. The forces of evil in this world are led by Satan, and he is actively working to destroy the people and work of Jesus Christ. He hates God and everyone who stands with God, and he is attacking the church, the home, and the personal lives of Christians to try to defeat them.

As believers we are part of God's army, called to do battle with the devil. But if we are not armed and equipped, with a battle plan and a clear line of communication to our Commander-in-Chief, we will be defeated. Satan is a shrewd and ruthless enemy, and if we are going to fight him we must be armed with the girdle of truth, the breastplate of right-eousness, the shoes of the gospel of peace, the shield of faith, and the helmet of salvation. We must have taken up the sword of the Spirit so that we have an offensive weapon with which to fight, and we must be constantly in prayer so that we have the mind of Christ with us at all times. Only then can we hope to defeat Satan and achieve victory.

This study will explore the spiritual battle we are in, and help you prepare for it. You will learn what each piece of armor is and how to appropriate it. You will also get to know your enemy, so you can see how he works and how you can defeat him. And, best of all, you will begin to develop a plan for achieving victory in your life.

Are We Really in a War?

Ephesians 6:10-18

OUTLINE

In this lesson we will be introduced to the concept of spiritual warfare.

I. **The Spiritual Battle**
II. **The Armor of God**
    A. The Girdle of Truth
    B. The Breastplate of Righteousness
    C. The Shoes of the Gospel of Peace
    D. The Shield of Faith
    E. The Helmet of Salvation
    F. The Sword of the Spirit
    G. All Prayer

OVERVIEW

Alexander Scriabin was one of the most controversial musical composers of his day. Born on Christmas Day in 1871, he won a gold medal at the Moscow Conservatory at the age of 21 and went on to compose and perform some of the most difficult piano pieces ever written. His early pieces are exquisite miniatures, possessing a harmony expressive of his vision of beauty. Scriabin toured Europe, returning to Moscow in 1898 as the youngest professor ever at the Conservatory. Then his life began to change.

The composer began dabbling in mysticism. His work started to portray darker themes. Friends said that he washed his hands hundreds of times each day because he felt dirty and evil, that he spoke of evil forces inside of him, and that he had a foreboding spirit of something terrible happening. Scriabin began having delusions of his own messianic importance, claimed that he was God, and eventually acknowledged that he was inspired by Satan. He died at the age of 44; his last words were, "This means the end. What a catastrophe!"

How strange that a man born on Christ's birthday ended up thinking he was God. Alexander Scriabin even imitated Jesus' actions by teaching men from a boat on a lake, describing himself as "light," and preaching his own message by attempting to replace faith in Christ with a celebration of Satan. Aping Christ, Scriabin was an anti-christ—filled with Satan, controlled by Satan, and ultimately destroyed by Satan.

People today don't want to believe in the devil anymore. Even many people who say they are Christians don't believe in the reality of Satan. But he is alive and well on planet earth, destroying the work of Jesus Christ whenever he can. Scripture plainly teaches this. In Ephesians 6:12 we are warned that we do not wrestle against flesh and blood, but against principalities and powers and rulers of darkness and spiritual wickedness in high places. That is a presentation of the domain of Satan. The forces of evil in this world are led by him, a great army of fallen angels that, according to the passage, are well organized into a hierarchy. "Principalities" in the Greek language means "head officers." "Powers" has to do with "staff officers." "Rulers" are "divisional commanders," and the rank and file are "spiritual hosts of wickedness."

The Spiritual Battle

In Ephesians 6:11 we are told that we are doing battle in every-day life against the wiles of the devil. The word "wiles" means "strategy" or "plans of war," so Satan is attacking the lives and causes of Christians. He is at war with those who would defeat his plans, which is why Christians feel so much of the effect of his presence. Satan is not after those who already belong to him; he is after those who want to defeat him. That is why we need to understand his efforts, as Paul wrote to the Corinthians, so that we are not ignorant of his devices.

The Bible says that Satan's purpose is to blind sinners and beguile Christians, and to hurt and discourage those who belong to God. He will do anything to disturb the mind, deceive the heart, and defeat life. He is actively involved in the world today, and if you read your Bible you'll find he has always been active. He led Lot into Sodom, got Peter to deny Christ, made Annanias and Sapphira lie to the church, and even dared attack Jesus Christ. If he isn't afraid to attack the Lord of Glory you should not be surprised to discover that he is willing to attack the most mature Christian. He wants to bring division into the church today, paralyzing its ministry and scandalizing its leaders.

The thing most often forgotten by Christians today is that we live on Satan's territory. We are not fighting on neutral ground, nor on God's ground. The battle we fight is fought on the enemy's territory. Christians today are fighting a war on foreign turf, and the world, the flesh, and the devil are our common enemies. They all maneuver in order to entice us and cause weakness and failure in our lives. So if we are going to fight in this war, we had better recognize that there really is a war going on and how it will be fought.

The devil has three primary goals, and it should be evident that he is at least moderately successful in each of his attacks. First, he is after every individual Christian to destroy his life. Second, he is after every Christian home to destroy its unity, its purity, and its oneness. Third, he is after every Christian church, to erode its ministry, discredit its leaders, wipe out its financial base, and destroy it so that it no longer has a presence in the world of darkness.

1 Peter 5:8 warns us: "Be sober, be vigilant because your adversary the devil walks about like a roaring lion, seeking whom he may devour." That succinctly sums up Satan's purpose in the world

today. He is looking for people to devour. He wants to devour your testimony. He seeks to devour your influence for Jesus Christ. He desires to find every little advantage he can get in your life with the ultimate purpose of devouring everything that could be used for Christ's purposes.

Recently the church went through a series of scandals, with famous television pastors having their secret sins exposed to the world. My heart broke for those men. They had a national presence in hundreds of thousands of homes all over the world and suddenly they were discredited because of their lifestyles. Satan got to them and destroyed their testimonies, devoured their influence, their success, their ability to be trusted. I have always been proud of being a minister of the gospel of Christ, but for a while all Christian pastors were embarrassed. Looking back, I have no condemnation. My task is to love God and His people, no matter what they do, and I don't want to be part of that controversy. But there is one truth of which I am absolutely certain: here were men of God who had great influence over many and were devoured by Satan. I doubt they will ever have that ability again, and it is because the devil worked to destroy them.

And this is exactly his goal for every single person who is a Christian. He delights every time it happens. If he can sow discord in your family and cause your home to break apart, or cause dissension in your family, he laughs with glee. He has achieved his goal. If he can get you to be divisive and critical and sow division among God's people, he has accomplished what he wants. His three-prong attack is the Christian, the home, and the church, and he is doing his job better than he has ever done it.

The Bible tells us that we are in a war, and the text says, "we wrestle." We are not wrestling against flesh and blood, but with a spiritual enemy. The term "wrestle" is one of great intensity. It pictures a man with a grip on another, pressing hard, straining every muscle to pin him to the ground. He uses all of his energy to resist. For the child of God it is the straining of every moral muscle, the testing of every spiritual sinew. We are not called as Christians to a time of relaxation in the summer's sun—we are called to a grim struggle with unseen forces—and the fight is real.

A.W. Tozer wrote at the closing of his ministry that "in the early days when Christianity exercised a dominant influence over American thinking, men conceived the world to be a battleground. Our fathers believed in sin, the devil, and hell as constituting one force, and they believed in God, righteousness, and heaven as the other." Man "could not be neutral... and if he chose to come out on God's side, he could expect open war with God's enemies." How different today! Tozer went on to say that in modern times "men think of the world not as a battleground, but a playground. We are not here to fight, but to frolic. We are not in a foreign land, we are home . . . and the best we can do is rid ourselves of our inhibitions and our frustrations and live this life here to the full." Tozer was right. We have lost the sense that we are at war and that is why we are so often defeated. It's not that Christians don't want to win. They don't even know they are at war!

The Armor of God

Yet the Word of God tells us that this warfare is one for which we may prepare. We can walk into a hostile environment and do warfare for God and not be defeated. Our Commander-in-Chief has already won the war, and He is waiting for us to get in on the victory. But you can't win unless you are armed. That's why Paul told the Ephesians, "Take up the whole armor of God." Note that Paul didn't tell us that God would bestow this armor on us. He told us to arm ourselves. It is your responsibility to appropriate the armor of God, and He gives us details about how to put it on. It is your job to do that. If you are shot at and defeated because you didn't put the armor in place, it is not God's fault. His armor is sitting there, waiting for you to put it on. It is your personal and primary duty to put on the armor of God, which will protect you from what the enemy wants to do to you.

The Girdle of Truth

Each piece of armor deals specifically with an area of your life that is a target of Satanic strategy. For example, the girdle of truth is the knowledge, acceptance, and use of truth. It consists of the great truths of God and His relationship to us through Christ. It includes a complete understanding about what God has said concerning Himself, His Son, mankind, and history. The girdle of truth is the knowledge of God which resides in His Word. To put on the girdle of truth you must know His Word. One of the ploys of Satan is to have cults feed off of ignorant Christian churches. Churches that don't know Biblical doctrine are unprotected from the seduction of strange teachings because they don't have on the armor of God.

Christian, take advantage of every opportunity to learn more about God and His Word so that you can be armed against the enemy who is out to destroy you. Put on the girdle of truth.

The Breastplate of Righteousness

Darts are aimed at your chest, and you need the protection of a breastplate. Satan is aiming to hurt you by attacking the sin in your life, and the breastplate of righteousness is the only thing that can protect you.

The Shoes of the Gospel of Peace

This has to do with witnessing to advance the cause of Christ. Did you know that your desire and willingness to witness is part of your protection against the enemy? That is because you never walk so close to the Lord as you do when you are trusting Him to give you courage to witness to those around you.

The Shield of Faith

Your shield protects you from the direct assault of the enemy. And your faith, your confidence in God's promises, becomes your shield in the spiritual battle.

The Helmet of Salvation

In battle, your helmet protects you from suffering a blow to your head and becoming dazed. Salvation changes your thinking process, and Christians have many teaching ministries to protect them against the intrusion of the immoral teachings of our day. It is your salvation relationship with Christ that protects your mind from Satan's evil influences.

The Sword of the Spirit

Scripture tells us to take in our hands an offensive weapon, the sword of the Spirit, which is the Word of God. Jesus used God's Word when He was tempted by Satan. Satan would offer an idea, and Jesus would reply, "It is written." That is using God's Word as a sword to defeat the enemy.

The Weapon of Prayer

What the long range ballistics missile is to the soldier, prayer is to the believer. All of the fighting is to be done in an atmosphere of prayer so that we are constantly in touch with our Commander. We are not to be cocky and put our confidence in the flesh, but

James 4:7-8 promises us that if we submit to God and resist the devil, he will flee from us. And the best news of all is that we are guaranteed to win, because Christ defeated the enemy on the cross. We are already victorious, and this study is about living the victory that God has guaranteed through Jesus Christ. Rather than becoming a casualty, God can help us to learn how to be victorious warriors in the great spiritual battle.

APPLICATION

1. What picture comes to mind when you hear the words "spiritual warfare"?

How do you respond to the idea that there is a spiritual battle going on between God's people and Satan's evil forces?

How can you get a feeling for a battle that is primarily spiritual?

2. What do you think it means to "be strong in the Lord and in His mighty power"?

3. According to Ephesians 6:10-12, who is our battle against?

Who is our battle not against?

Why is the distinction significant?

What do these verses reveal about our enemy?

4. When have you felt spiritually strong?

Describe a time you felt spiritually defeated.

Why do you think we experience these times?

5. Why do we need armor?

How does spiritual armor help us?

Which pieces of armor do you feel you are using?

Where do you feel the most vulnerable? Why?

6. Paul encourages his readers to "stand firm" four times in verses 11-14.

What does that reveal about the battle?

What does it reveal about the use of God's resources?

Why do we sometimes find it hard to "stand firm"?

DID YOU KNOW?

When Paul wrote the letter to the Ephesians, he was in prison and chained to a Roman soldier (see Ephesians 6:20). The soldier was charged with staying with Paul at all times. His description of our spiritual armor was based upon the very real armor his guard was wearing, and his use of military terms doubtless reveals the kind of conversation Paul was having with those around him.

Identifying the Enemy

Ephesians 6:10-13

OUTLINE

In this lesson we will learn to know our enemy, his strategies, and what our response should be.

I. **Our Enemy**
  A. Satan's Personality
  B. Satan's Position
  C. Satan's Power
  D. Satan's Purposes
  E. Satan's Strategies
II. **Our Challenge**

OVERVIEW

The devil's cleverest ruse is to make believe that he does not exist. That's why there are so many ridiculous pictures of him dressed in horns and a red suit, sporting a tail and an evil grin. If he is a comic figure, there is apparently little harm he can do.

His disguises are also clever. He hides in religion, art, intellectualism, education, philosophy, and psychology. He has been called the original jet-setter, always at work in the latest cause. The Lord once asked him, "From where do you come?" Satan replied, "From going to and fro on the earth" (Job 2:2). Roaming the earth, looking for ways to turn people from God, that is the true picture of Satan. He is real, and he is the enemy.

Our Enemy

Paul tells us in Ephesians 6 that the Christian is in a war against Satan. He uses the word "against" five times in describing the battle. We are against Satan, and he is against us—strong words for a culture that has adopted a passivist attitude about the Christian life. In recent years many denominations decided to remove all of the militant hymns from their hymnbooks. "Onward Christian Soldiers" has been dropped in a desire to remove the idea that there is a fight being waged. For them, Christianity is about peace and love, and they want to do away with the concept of spiritual warfare.

Yet it is unhealthy to believe there is no conflict in the Christian life, because the world is full of conflict. One scholar has translated 6:13 this way: "For our contest is not with human foes alone, but with rulers, authorities, and cosmic powers of this dark world. That is, the spirit forces of evil challenging us in the heavenly contest." You see, Satan is our enemy, and we are his enemy. That is why Paul's instruction to the Ephesians in verse 10 is, "Finally, my brethren, be strong." This isn't just a war for the apostles or the pastors, but for all the brethren. Every one of us is involved in the battle, and it goes on every day in your life, my life, and the world.

The battle lines are drawn up. God and his people are on one side, Satan and his demons on the other. Scripture identifies the enemy as "the devil" (in verse 11) and "the wicked one" (verse 16). And no one goes to war without learning all he can about the one he expects to fight. Countries spend millions of dollars on intelligence agencies to keep the government informed on the character and activities of their enemies. One of the principles of war is that you "know your enemy," so let's take a look at the one against whom we fight.

Satan's Personality

Satan is the most bitter enemy of God and His people. Even his names tell you of his personality. He is called in Scripture "the deceiver" (Revelation 12:9), "a murderer" (John 8:44), "a tempter" (Matthew 4:3), "the destroyer" which means destruction (Revelation 9:11), "the liar" (John: 8:44) "the accuser of the brethren" (Revelation 12:10), and "the evil one" (1 John 5:19). He is depicted as a roaring lion, searching the world for those he can devour, yet he attempts to portray himself as an "angel of light" (2 Corinthians 11:14). From generation to generation he continues his attack. He is the arch traitor against God.

Originally he was different. Strange as it may seem, he was originally God's cherished creation. In Isaiah 14 and Ezekiel 28 you can read about the earlier days of Satan. He was called Lucifer, "The son of the morning," "the shining one," and "the day star." Ezekiel 28 reveals he was "the anointed cherub;" perfect in beauty and in all of his ways full of wisdom; gifted with marvelous intelligence and glorious in holiness.

So, what happened? How did Lucifer cease to be the son of the morning and become Satan, arch-enemy of God? Ezekiel 28 reveals that Lucifer lifted up his heart with pride, which led to self-exaltation and rebellion against God. Isaiah 14:12-13 says, "How you are fallen from heaven, O Lucifer, son of the morning! . . . For you have said in your heart, 'I will ascend into heaven, I will exalt my throne above the stars of God; I will sit on the mount of the congregation. . . I will ascend above the heights of the clouds. I will be like the Most High.'" When those words came out of his mouth, sin began in the universe, and he was cast out of his position. Cast down as a profane one from the mountain of God, he was brought down into hell, taking many angels with him.

I don't pretend to understand all of the theological implications of that, but clearly God allowed His angels a choice, and they worship before His throne to this day because they choose to do so. But Satan, in his own heart, chose to lift himself up in pride, bringing about his own downfall. Ever since he was cast out of his original position, he has organized rebellion against God. He is angry, scheming, and spiteful, and he has put in place a system to wage war with God. His personality is one of pride and hatred toward God and everything that is good and holy.

Satan's Position

The Bible gives Satan three names that reveal his position. First, it calls him a prince. He is "the prince of this world" (John 12:31) and "the prince of the power of the air" (Ephesians 2:2). As such he is the ruler of evil men and evil spirits. He is the one behind all the evil in the world today.

Second, the Bible calls him a ruler in charge of his own kingdom. He is the power behind our world system. When you see intrigue, aggression, brutality, ambition, greed, and a lust for power, you are seeing the results of the personal system of Satan.

The third name given Satan in Scripture is god—he is the god of this age (2 Corinthians 4:4). As an imposter and imitator he wants to set himself up like the true God, so he has instituted his own religion. That's why the writers of the New Testament refer to the synagogue of Satan (Revelation 2:9), his ministers (2 Corinthians 11), and his gospel (Galatians 1). He even has his own communion table and cup (1 Corinthians 10:20-21). He is the god of this age, presiding over his own religion.

Satan's Power

He is the second most powerful person in the universe, subject only to God. It is good for Christians to remember and respect this enemy, for he has the power to destroy. The Bible says that men are held captive by that power until delivered by the power of the Savior. He is associated with the power of darkness, the power of the air, and the power of death. He is defined as both a roaring lion and a great dragon, and is described as diabolical, deceptive, destructive, rebellious, and filled with hate. He has his own armor, strongholds, and strongman, and is a very powerful enemy.

Satan's Purposes

Having been cast out of his original position, the devil is filled with fury and envy. His anger is directed against God and His people. His aim is to defeat God by throwing people into hell. Satan wants all people destroyed and in hell, so he travels the earth as a roaring lion bent on destroying people. He has a well-organized army fighting for him, and they set up an outpost in the heart of every person to keep them in bondage to sin.

One of the reasons so many prominent Christians have fallen into sin in recent years is because they have underestimated the enemy and have not done battle with that outpost of sin in their lives. Satan uses that area of sin as a beachhead from which he can expand into more territory until he has destroyed the believer's life, which is his purpose. Christian, you are in a life and death battle!

Satan's Strategies

Have you ever noticed the number of verbs associated with Satan? He beguiles, seduces, opposes, resists, deceives, hinders, buffets, tempts, and persecutes believers. Look at some of the strategies he uses to try and destroy our lives.

The great deceiver, Satan, tries to copy everything God has. He has a counterfeit church and someday will offer a counterfeit savior called the Anti-Christ. He is always trying to deceive people into believing a lie. John 8:44 says that "there is no truth in him. When he speaks a lie, he speaks from his own resources." Satan is the father of all lies. Lying is his native tongue. His first ploy was to deceive Eve, and he is at work today through false teachers and false prophets who misquote Scripture, teach corruption, and mix just enough truth with falsehood to seem trustworthy and believable. He deceives people into believing he doesn't exist, convinces them that good can come from evil, and even misleads people in believing their sin "isn't really that bad."

Satan is the great divider. His first act after falling from grace was to divide the angels. He divided the first family so that brother killed brother. He has worked to divide churches and denominations by sowing suspicion, intolerance, criticism, and dislike among Christians. One of his chief strategies is to divide and conquer.

Satan is the great destroyer. Scripture calls Satan "Apollyon" (Revelation 9:11), which means "the destroyer." He wants to destroy your life through adversity, getting in the way and blocking the moves that God wants to make in your life. He does that by discouragement, by dissipating your time and energy, and by a frontal assault on your weak areas to lead you to sin. Satan wants to disrupt your walk with God, ruin your testimony, and destroy your life.

Our Challenge

That is our enemy. There you have his personality, his position, and his power. Some of you are probably saying, "What a discouraging study. I wish I'd never started this! What am I supposed to do?" Well, that is good! I hope you are overwhelmed with this enemy to the point where you are taking him seriously. I hope you are aware of the spiritual battle being waged, because you can't do anything about him. You are absolutely outmanned, and if you try to do battle in your own power you are already defeated because he is stronger than you. In fact, the only power you have against the enemy is the power you have in Jesus Christ.

Look at Ephesians 6:10: "Finally, my brethren, be strong in the Lord and in the power of His might. Put on the whole armor of God." You can't fight Satan in the flesh, because that leads to so much defeat and discouragement. You get this idea that "I just need to try harder," and you wind up being defeated. People who lived generations before us understood the spiritual battle, and they recognized the role of God's power. That's why those militant hymns were originally written! That's why Martin Luther could write, "A mighty fortress is our God, a bulwark never failing. Our helper He, amid the flood of mortal ills prevailing. For still our ancient foe doth seek to work us woe; his craft and power are great, and armed with cruel hate, on earth is not his equal. Did we in our own strength confide, our striving would be losing. Were not the right Man on our side, the Man of God's own choosing. Dost ask who that may be? Christ Jesus, it is He. Lord Sabbaoth His name, from age to age the same, and He must win the battle."

You cannot fight the fight in your own strength, but praise God, He has given us the armor that provides for our defense, and the sword that we use in offense. As one hymn writer put it:

Stand up, stand up for Jesus,
Stand in His strength alone.
The arm of flesh will fail you,
You dare not trust your own.
Put on the gospel armor
And watching unto prayer,
Where duty calls, or danger,
Be never wanting there.

APPLICATION

1. Look at Ezekiel 28:12-17 and Isaiah 14:12-14. Where did Satan come from?

How did he fall?

What was his sin, and how does that relate to us?

2. Why is it important to learn who Satan is and how he operates?

How can that information help you in your spiritual battle?

How do you fight Satan?

3. According to Job 1:6-11 and 2:1-5, what does Satan do?

How does this relate to 1 Peter 5:8?

How is the character of Satan described in the following passages:

Matthew 13:19

John 8:44

John 12:31

2 Corinthians 4:4

2 Corinthians 11:14

Ephesians 2:2

2 Thessalonians 2:9

Hebrews 2:14

4. Several verses of Scripture refer to Satan's "church." What can you discover about his church from the following passages:

1 Corinthians 10:20-21

2 Corinthians 11:3-4 & 13-15

1 Timothy 4:1

Revelation 2:9

5. In what ways do you see Satan trying to deceive people today?

How does Satan work to create divisions in the church?

What can a church do to fight back?

How is Satan working to try and destroy your life?

What can you do to win the war?

6. Explore Matthew 25:41 and Revelation 20:1-3, 10 to find out what happens to Satan at the end of time.

What confidence does this give us?

What assurance does Romans 8:38-39 offer those in battle?

DID YOU KNOW?

For all his power, Satan is neither omnipotent, omniscient, nor omnipresent. His power has limitations, and he can only act within the limits imposed upon him by God. God is greater than Satan and his evil, which will never be able to separate Christians from God's love. He is permitted to afflict us, and God even uses him as a tool at times (1 Corinthians 5:5), but we can be assured that he will never have complete victory over us (John 16:33).

The Girdle of Truth

Ephesians 6:14

OUTLINE

In this lesson we will learn about the first piece of spiritual armor, the girdle of truth.

I. What is the Girdle?
II. Why is it used?
III. How do we use it?

OVERVIEW

Twice in Ephesians 6 we are told to "put on the whole armor of God." In verse 11 we are told to put it on so that we might stand against the wiles of the devil, and in verse 13 we are urged to put on the armor so "that you may be able to withstand in the evil day, and having done all, to stand." There are six pieces of armor in the list, each of which is a source of strength and security in warfare. Five of the pieces are defensive, one is offensive. We are not to choose which pieces we want to use; we are to put them all on. No part of our life may be left unguarded or exposed. Any piece we refuse to use will leave us vulnerable and cause us to be prey to the enemy.

Scripture tells us to clothe ourselves with this armor for defensive protection against Satan, who wants to destroy our testimonies and our lives. And since it is armor for fighting, note that God has provided no protection for the back. He expects no deserters in His army. He wants us all to stand and face the enemy and not run away as cowards. We are at war, and we must fight in the battle.

As we look at the armor it becomes quite apparent that it is nothing less than Christ Himself. In fact, when Paul wrote to the Romans he told them to "put on the Lord Jesus Christ," as he told the Ephesians to "put on the full armor of God." Is essence Paul is telling us to wear Christ just as we wear a suit of clothes. Clothes are with us all the time, always visible, and become a natural part of our lives. So also should Christ be always a part of our everyday living. When we put on the armor, we are putting on Christ and going forward in His strength to do battle.

The Bible tells us the responsibility for putting on the armor belongs to us. One writer put it: "He makes the armor, the Christian takes the armor." You are never told to wait for God to put it on you. It is your responsibility to implement it. You put it on yourself, for you are involved in a personal battle with Satan. Can you imagine a soldier waiting for his general to fasten his helmet, tie his shoes, and put bullets in his gun? The spiritual battle is huge, but it is also personal. You fight it individually, and if you do not personally implement the warrior's armor you will certainly fall in battle. It is your personal and primary duty to implement the armor of God, and to do so continually. You don't put it on once and it stays on forever—you must arm yourself regularly for the battle by appropriating the resources of God.

What is the Girdle?

The first piece of armor that we are to put on is the girdle of truth. Paul says, "Stand therefore, having girded your waist with truth." It's really rather strange that the apostle would start with the girdle, or that he should even mention the girdle, because Roman soldiers did not even consider it a piece of their armor. In fact, the girdle was a common piece of dress worn by almost all Romans, whether warrior or not. It was usually a six-inch belt that fastened around the middle, made of either leather or linen. It was worn outside the long, flowing robe that was commonly worn in Paul's day, and it had a specific purpose. If you read your Bible carefully you will find verses that say, "Gird up your loins," and you may wonder what the author means. When a Roman was interested in moving from one place to another rapidly, he would take his long robe, pull it up, and tuck it into his girdle. That way the robe would not encumber him when he was running or moving quickly. When a soldier from the Roman garrison was sent into battle he would do the same thing, tucking his robe into the girdle around his waist so that he would not trip over it or get it caught on something in battle.

Why is it used?

Paul tells the Ephesians that they are to put on the girdle of truth as the first thing to prepare for battle. It is a reminder that Christians are going to go into battle, so they had best take that first step and prepare. The writer of Hebrews strikes a similar theme when he says, "Let us lay aside every weight, and the sin that so easily ensnares us, and let us run the race that is set before us" Hebrew 12:1. Before going to do battle, the first thing a soldier does is prepare for the rest of his armor by utilizing his girdle. Now he will not be tripped up, and he is ready to prepare for the fight.

The girdle was also used by the soldier as the place where he supported his weapons. The swordsman hung his sword from it; the bowman used it to support his quiver of arrows. The girdle was strong enough to bind the clothing together and support the offensive weapons with which the soldier fought.

The Roman soldier would also pin his award on that belt. If he was a decorated soldier, he would have his medallion pinned to it so that those who saw him would know what sort of man they were dealing with. This was not just any soldier, but a distinguished fighter for the Roman Empire.

It is interesting that this primary piece of clothing is called "the girdle of truth." Truth is at the very foundation of the Christian life. Jesus called Satan "the father of all lies," and the Bible says there is no truth in him. Our enemy's primary attack will be as a deceiver, trying to entangle us with falsehoods and half-truths so that we become confused. The devil wants to keep us from walking in integrity, so he will try to misinform and upset us so that we get bogged down in sin. The way to deal with the deceiver is to implement God's truth in our lives. Christ, the Truth and the true God, is our armor against the attacks of Satan.

Jesus said in John 14:6, "I am the way, the truth. . ." He is the ultimate truth, and when we arm ourselves with Him we are ready to face the lies and confusion of the enemy.

How we use it?

How do we arm ourselves with the truth? By knowing the truth! In order to do battle, the believer needs to know the truth about God, the truth about Christ, and the truth embodied in His holy Word, the Bible. Christ Himself, when encountered by Satan in the wilderness, did battle by using the truth. When Satan tempted him, Christ fought back with the doctrine of Scripture by noting, "It is written" and quoting an appropriate passage (Matthew 4:1-11). And when Satan tried to twist Scripture by quoting a verse out of context, Jesus responded with a truthful understanding of that passage. You see, when you put on the truth you are understanding what the Bible says about God.

This is a clear call for Christian men and women to know their doctrine. People are afraid of the word "doctrine," but it simply means "systematized truth." Doctrine is the truth of the Word of God organized and categorized so that we can think clearly about the issues of life. For us to be armed with the truth means that we take God's truth, organize it, systematize it, and memorize it so that when the enemy attacks us there is a body of truth at hand with which we can fight back. You can use your knowledge of Scripture to battle Satan the same way Jesus did.

The lack of understanding and teaching doctrine has made the ignorance of Christians all the more glaring, and helps to explain why so many warriors are falling these days. It is possible to live the

Christian life just on the surface, knowing only enough to carry on an intelligent conversation in the church foyer with another equally uninformed believer. But when that happens you are vulnerable to the attack of the deceiver.

God expects us to learn the truth. That is one of the reasons you go to church, study his Word, and participate in a small group. The sermon is not for entertainment, but for arming people with the truth. God has called us to teach the Bible. If His people will put on the girdle of truth, and make the pursuit of God the focus of their Christian walk, Satan will meet some big defeats.

Paul's desire for the churches to whom he ministered was that they arm themselves with truth. That's why he prayed in Ephesians 1 that God "may give to you the spirit of wisdom and revelation in the knowledge of Him, the eyes of your understanding being enlightened; that you may know what is the hope of His calling, what are the riches of the glory of His inheritance in the saints, and what is the exceeding greatness of His power toward us who believe." Paul wanted the Ephesians to be armed with the truth. He wanted them to understand that God's truth is eternal and useful in the spiritual battle we all face. When you are feeling discouraged, confused, or defeated, you had better know how to fight back with the Word of God. You need to gird up the loins of your mind by way of the truth of God.

You not only need to know the truth, you need to live the truth. The child of God who goes into battle must have integrity of character. That gives him the courage and confidence to do battle with the enemy. Nothing so demoralizes a warrior than to know the cause he fights for is unjust and untrue. Nothing will discourage you more than attempting to do warfare with Satan when there is a problem of character in your life. Outwardly things may look fine, but inwardly you are harboring sin and unfaithfulness to God, and you can bet Satan will find your weak spot and attack it.

When you do battle with Satan, there are no pretenders. There is no faking it. You have to be real from the inside out. Perhaps one of the reasons the church suffers so today is that many Christians know how to fake their walk with Christ. They can "talk the talk" but can't "walk the walk." And after faking it for so long, they begin to think that their fantasy is reality. They mistake their immaturity for maturity, their carnality for spirituality, and that allows Satan to destroy them. They go to do battle unprepared for a fierce attack, and are exposed and defeated as unarmed soldiers. The sword, the only offensive part of our armor, hangs from our belt. You cannot use the sword, which is the Word of God, effectively unless the Word is evident in your life. You will get tripped up, just as a soldier without a girdle would trip on his own robe.

We do not live our lives simply so people will think well of us. We are to live our lives to please God, and He knows who is real. Christ illustrated this in His own life. When accused, He asked, "Which one of you convicts Me of sin?" No one could respond, for He was without sin. Jesus Christ was girded about with the girdle of truth. That is why Paul urged young pastors to minister with a clear conscience. If there is something wrong in their lives and they haven't dealt with it, the enemy will defeat them in battle. So you put on this first piece of armor before going into battle. You don't wait until the bullets are flying overhead to get dressed. Take time to examine your life. See if you know the truth and are living it out.

APPLICATION

1. Why is it important to be a person marked by truth?

How does a reputation for truthfulness impact a person's life?

Conversely, what does a reputation for a lack of truthfulness lead to?

2. Read through 3 John. What does John mean when he writes that they "continue to walk in truth" (verse 3)?

Re-write verse 4 in your own words.

What does John suggest is the motivation for Christian caring in verse 8?

In verses 9-12 he compares two men, Diotrephes and Demetrius. What marks each man's life?

3. What do the following Psalms teach us about being girded by truth?

Psalm 25:4-5

Psalm 26:1-8

Psalm 51:6

Psalm 86:11

Psalm 119:160

Psalm 145:18

4. How does God's truth protect us? (see Psalm 40:11)

How does God's truth guide us? (see Psalm 43:3)

What does it mean to "worship the Father in truth"? (John 4:23-24)

5. Who is the most truthful person you know? How do you respond to him/her?

What do other people think of him/her?

Could it be said that your life is marked by truth? Why or why not?

According to 1 John 2:3-6 & 20-23, how should the people of God live out the truth?

6. What do the following verses from John's writings tell us about God, Christ, and the Holy Spirit?

John 1:17

John 3:21

John 8:32

John 14:6

John 14:16-17

John 16:13

John 17:17

John 18:37

1 John 1:5-8

7. How can a person appropriate the girdle of truth?

What benefit will accrue to you by wearing the girdle of truth into the spiritual battle?

DID YOU KNOW?

In Paul's day merchants sold pottery under the word "Sine Cerus." It means "without wax" and it referred to the fact that unscrupulous merchants would rub beeswax into the cracks of broken pottery to sell to unsuspecting customers. But honest merchants would advertise their crockery as "without wax," inviting customers to inspect the merchandise closely for flaws. The English language still uses those Latin words to refer to people who are honest, whose lives we can inspect and find no pretense. The word, as we now say it, is "sincere," and that describes Christians whose lives are girded by truth.

The Breastplate of Righteousness

Ephesians 6:14

OUTLINE

In this lesson we will learn about the piece of armor that protects our hearts.

   I. Christ's Righteousness
  II. The Christian's Righteousness
 III. Consistent Righteousness
 IV. Controlled Righteousness

OVERVIEW

When I was a student in seminary, studying for the ministry, I decided not to do battle with Satan. It wasn't a conscious decision, mind you, but every day I was dealing with the truth of God's Word and the principles in it, and I got so comfortable talking about it that I forgot that I needed to apply it to my life. My wife and I went to a huge church, always arriving late. Nobody knew we were there. Nobody knew if we weren't there, either. We could slip in, hear some great preaching, then slip out, totally uninvolved. I was studying the Bible for classes, but not appropriating it into my life. Someone has said that there are two kinds of pillars in the church: the strong pillars that hold the church together, and the caterpillars who crawl in and out each Sunday. We were representatives of the people who don't want to be in the battle, and I believe that's where a majority of believers are today. So I had to ask myself a couple questions: Do I care about this spiritual battle? Do I really want to fight in it?

There are many Christians who cannot answer in the affirmative. They are glad to go to church, happy to sit in the pew, want to feel good about being a Christian, but have no desire to fight in the battle for Christ. They don't have the girdle of truth wrapped around them with a purposeful desire to be soldiers. But for those who have made that decision, who have a sincere desire to wage war with Satan, the next step in preparing for battle is to put on the breastplate of righteousness.

Several years ago I read about James Kennedy's work on evangelism. I shall never forget my surprise when I read the results of a nationwide survey that asked Christians, "Why don't you witness?" I anticipated the answers would be "I'm afraid," or "I don't know how," or even "I don't know any unsaved people." None of those answers made the top five. What was the most popular answer? It was: "I don't witness because of the life that I live." That answer gets right to the heart of what it means to wear the breastplate of righteousness.

A breastplate was the piece of armor that covered the body from the neck to the thighs. It consisted of two parts, the front was one solid piece, and the other piece went over the shoulders and had straps that crossed in back, cinching it tight against your body. The warrior, without his breastplate, was dangerously exposed to the enemy and could easily be killed because his vital organs were left unprotected. An arrow to the heart or a sword to the bowels would immediately snuff out his life.

When we are told as believers to put on the breastplate of righteousness, it is obviously not a physical thing we are to do but a spiritual, symbolic act. Putting on your breastplate of righteousness involves several ideas.

Christ's Righteousness

The Bible tells us that when we become Christians, we are immediately equipped with the righteousness of Christ. Paul told the Corinthians, "But of Him you are in Christ Jesus, who became for us wisdom from God—and righteousness, and sanctification, and redemption (1 Corinthians 1:30)." When Jesus Christ came down to this earth as the perfect Son of God, He went to the cross and died for you.

As He hung upon the cross two major things happened. First, He took our sin upon Himself. The Bible says He became sin for us. All the sins of the world were crucified on that cross with Jesus. Second, He imparted righteousness to us. So when we give our lives over to Him, when we put our trust in Him for eternal life, Christ not only forgives our sin but gives to us His righteousness. We become righteous in Christ Jesus.

You know, that is the greatest bargain the world has ever known. You give up your sin and you get His righteousness in return. I have never been able to understand why people turn that down. It is the greatest opportunity anybody has ever had, to get rid of your sin and get the righteousness of Christ imputed to your account in return. That is exactly what happened, and that is why Paul writes, "and be found in Him, not having my own righteousness, which is from the law, but that which is through faith in Christ, the righteousness which is from God by faith" (Philippians 3:9).

When you put on the breastplate of righteousness, it symbolizes the fact that you are protected by the righteousness of Christ. When the old accuser goes before the Lord and points out all your faults and foibles, God just answers, "I don't see that person the same way. I see him through my Son, Jesus Christ, and when I look I see a righteous person." That is your armor, and you don't have to worry about Satan accusing you before the Father because when the Lord looks at you, He sees Christ and His righteousness. Doesn't that just make you want to praise God?

The Christian's Righteousness

Too many Christians accept their position in Christ and do little about their practice. They are saved but not practicing their sanctification. That is, they have not become in practice what they are in position. They want to put on some armor on the inside, but they don't want to wear the armor on the outside. They want to live careless, worldly, indifferent lives and then excuse themselves with, "Well, before God I'm righteous." The breastplate of righteousness symbolizes not only the righteousness of Christ, but the righteousness of Christians. If we are righteous in Christ up in heaven's eyes, we should be righteous down here before the eyes of the world. It is a wretched business to go your own way, live in the flesh, and then sing the hymn "Faultless Before the Throne I Stand." Your position in Christ needs to be reflected in your practice.

The breastplate of righteousness is ours; therefore we should live according to the pattern of the Word of God. We can stand before the temptations of Satan without yielding if we know we are living righteous lives. The Bible says we are to put on righteousness. Ephesians 4:24 says, "that you put on the new man which was according to God, created in true righteousness and holiness." It does not say to wait for God to put it on. It doesn't tell you to stand around until it comes. It tells you to put it on. Begin to live in practice what you already are in position.

When we get to heaven we will be wearing our righteousness. The book of Revelation tells us that we will be clothed in the white raiment of our righteous lives. For some Christians, that's going to be nigh on indecent exposure! Apart from righteousness, the Christian has no defense against Satan's accusations. So you are dead if you don't live a righteous life. You're an easy target. Satan will come and make you doubt whether you are even a Christian. You will have to defend against his attacks. The testimony of your lips will be ineffective, because like the people in James Kennedy's survey, you will think, "How can I tell others what Christ has done for me when my life isn't any different from their lives?" Your neighbor down the street won't want Christ because he won't see in you what you claim to have in Christ. The reason we are losing this war is because too many Christians want to cozy up to the world, live comfortably in the culture, and not really fight the battle against Satan.

But keep in mind that if you really don't want to fight this war, you shouldn't be complaining when you lose. If you are not willing to put on the breastplate of righteousness, you have no cause for whining about your defeat and the devil's victory in your life. You have never even entered the fray.

Consistent Righteousness

Please don't misunderstand me. In the flesh it is impossible to be righteous. If we could be, Christ would not have had to die. But it is possible to wear the armor of righteousness consistently. In 2 Corinthians 6:3-10 Paul describes the righteous life of the believer by saying, "give no offense in anything, that our ministry may not be blamed. But in all things we commend ourselves as ministers of God: in much patience, in tribulations, in needs, in distresses, in stripes, in imprisonments, in tumults, in labors, in sleeplessness, in fastings; by purity, by knowledge, by long-suffering, by kindness, by the Holy Spirit, by sincere love, by the word of truth, by the power of God, by the armor of righteousness." The Christian wearing the breastplate of righteousness has been changed by the power of God. He is godly in every situation. In times of stress, times of joy, and times of sorrow, you can discern that he is different. He isn't part of the world, but stands apart. His life is attractive, and when he speaks you listen because you know he has a unique quality about his life. That person has power in his life, in his witness, and in the conflict.

If you are not living righteously, you are just another easy target for Satan. I have been down that road, and I know what it's like. You harbor sin, so you can't seem to get things right with God. You can't witness, because you know your life doesn't match your words. You can't be victorious over temptation, for every time you try to do battle, the enemy brings to mind that spot in your life and you feel defeated. It is going into war without armor. But when you put on the breastplate of righteousness, you stand protected, confident that your heart is secure from the evil one. Dr. Charles Eerdman once said, "One who binds himself about with a determined loyalty to the holy will and law of God is secure against the deadly thrusts of the Tempter. A man who is conscious of being in the wrong is usually a coward. A man who knows that he is right can withstand a multi-tude and he enters the conflict without fear." There is nothing like knowing you are right with God to give you power in battle.

This will require some self-examination, so that you continually put on the breastplate. It isn't a one-time thing, or even a once-a-week activity to be done on the way to church every Sunday. Righteousness is something we must decide to live out every day of the week if we are going to fight in the battle.

Controlled Righteousness

The significance of the breastplate of righteousness is not only what it is, but what it protects. The breastplate basically is worn to protect the heart. It stops an enemy's arrow from piercing your heart and taking your life. The significance is that the heart represents your emotions and feelings. Consider, for example, that when you get angry your face gets red because the heart is pumping extra blood. When you get scared your face gets white because your heart grows faint and fails to pump enough blood. And when you fall in love, or when you fail in love, you feel it in your heart. Your heart is the seat of your emotions, and it needs to be protected from Satan.

Instead of walking around trying to be a better Christian, you need to let your heart fall in love with Jesus again. Instead of trying to do better in your Christian walk, you need to learn to love God more. When you learn to love the Lord through His Word, through prayer, through worship, and through interaction and accountability with other Christians, it will change your life. You won't be running around trying to figure out how to change your life and "be righteous." You will simply be so in love with the Lord that you will want to live to please Him. The old things will begin to fall away, and you will be renewed from the inside out. Instead of trying to control your life by your own power, you will begin to see the love of God controlling you. Love brings two together, and when you love God you want to live as God wants you to live.

When you put on the breastplate of righteousness, you are dealing with your heart. Where is your heart today? Too many Christians are more concerned with the pleasures and treasures of this world, rather than setting their heart on God. But by setting your heart on God, and living out His righteousness, you become powerful and protected in the spiritual war.

APPLICATION

1. What would your reply be if you were part of the survey asking "Why don't you witness?"?

Are there people close to you with whom you won't talk about spiritual things? Why?

Do you think people can see that Christ is in your life?

2. What does Christ mean when, in Matthew 5:6, He speaks of hungering and thirsting after righteousness?

Have you ever known anyone who hungered and thirsted after righteousness? What were they like?

3. What principle do you draw from Matthew 6:1?

How do you reconcile that with Paul's teaching to "put on righteousness"?

According to Romans 3:21-31, how do we obtain righteousness?

How do we practice our righteousness?

4. What do the following verses tell us about our righteousness?

Matthew 6:33

Romans 1:16-17

Romans 5:17

Romans 10:1-4

1 Corinthians 1:30

2 Corinthians 5:21

1 Timothy 6:11

2 Timothy 2:22

1 Peter 2:24

1 John 3:7-8

5. How can you be confident that you have the righteousness of Christ?

What do we do about our sin? (see 1 John 1:5-10)

What does God do about our sin, according to 1 John 2:1-2?

Read through Romans 7:7-25 and describe how Paul struggled with his sin.

In your own words, how do we put on righteousness without simply fighting Satan in our own power? (See Galatians 5:16-26)

6. What principles for living in righteousness do you find in Romans 6:15-20?

What does John urge us to do in 1 John 2:28-29?

How can you put these passages into practice?

7. What areas do you need to work on in putting on the breastplate of righteousness?

How does Satan attack you in those areas?

What can you do to arm yourself against his attacks?

DID YOU KNOW?

The breastplates of soldiers were commonly copper, brass, iron, or tin hammered to individually fit each man. They were lined with leather, so that when fighting in hot weather the metal didn't burn the skin. Some breastplates had high collars to protect the neck, and flaps to cover the groin. Those made of mail were like a cloth of woven chain links. These were extremely heavy, and could only be worn for relatively short periods without taxing the soldier. Buckets of water had to be kept close to the battle lines to pour on soldiers wearing mail, to keep them from suffering heat exhaustion. Breastplates proved extremely effective. Bullet-proof vests worn by modern policemen are simply an updated version of the breastplate.

The Shoes of the Gospel of Peace

Ephesians 6:15

OUTLINE

I n this lesson we will examine the gospel and its place in helping us stand firm for Christ.

I. The Relationship of the Shoes to the Armor
II. The Requirement of the Shoes for Armor
III. The Reasons for the Shoes as Armor
  A. Without Shoes, You Are Ungrateful
  B. Without Shoes, You Are Unreasonable
  C. Without Shoes, You Are Unproductive
  D. Without Shoes, You Are Unchristian
  E. Without Shoes, You Are Unprepared
IV. The Requisitioning of Shoes for Armor

OVERVIEW

Years ago I watched basketball player Kevin McHale lose a shoe during an NBA playoff game. Instead of stopping the game, he tossed his shoe off the court and continued playing. Of course the other team immediately threw the ball to the player McHale was guarding, and he got an easy bucket. You can't play basketball well without shoes, and according to the Bible, you can't fight the spiritual battle without shoes either.

Shoes are absolutely essential to fighting. Can you imagine a soldier all dressed up in his armor with no shoes on? He might be well-equipped in every other area, but without shoes he is unfit for fighting. His feet simply could not hold up to the rigors of hand-to-hand combat. Apart from some guerrillas, there are not very many barefoot soldiers.

Roman soldiers, about whom Paul was writing, wore hob-nailed sandals. They were specifically designed to be surefooted in battle. They had a thick base, made of wood and leather, and often had short spikes imbedded in them to give the soldier extra traction on inclines or in bad weather. Even on the slickest ground they could stand in hand-to-hand combat and not slip. Paul used this concept of Roman warfare, being properly shod when going into battle, to remind us of the importance of having a firm foundation.

The Scriptures say that the shoes we wear are the gospel of peace. In other words, we are to be prepared with the good news of peace. The foundation of our fighting in the spiritual battle is the settled peace within us that God wants us to have. You see, Satan is the destroyer of peace. His purpose in coming to earth was to bring division between man and separation from God. His first act was to cause a division between the angles. So when we do combat with him we need to have an implement of warfare that will enable us to withstand that particular attack of division and restlessness. The implements to use, according to Ephesians 6:15, are the shoes of the gospel of peace.

The Relationship of the Shoes to the Armor

Remember that the whole imagery of Ephesians 6 is that the believer needs to literally equip himself with Jesus Christ. He is to put on the Lord Jesus, and in the power of Christ, go forward into battle. Begin by putting on the girdle of truth, which is Christ. Then, put on the breastplate of righteousness, which is living according to that truth, protected from the enemy's arrows. Living out the truth leads to peace, which is what Paul is speaking about in verse 15. You start with the truth, which brings you to righteousness, which leads to peace. You are no longer struggling to prove yourself to God; He has declared you righteous in Jesus Christ.

So the relationship of the shoes to the rest of the armor is very logical. Remember, we are not in a battle against people. We are in a battle against the realm of thoughts and attitudes, and so it is important that we are equipped with inner peace from God. Much of the spiritual battle takes place in the realm of your outlook on life. It is not the situation in which you find yourself that is critical, but how you look on that situation in the power of Christ. We are to remember that in Jesus Christ we have peace. Ephesians 2:14 says, "He Himself is our peace." As we appropriate that truth into our lives, we can go out into the battle and be victorious.

During the darkest days of World War II, Londoners would turn on their radios and listen to the voice of one man ringing out over the airwaves. Winston Churchill's voice was strong and inspirational, and he strengthened the morale of the British time and time again. That is what Jesus does for us. He comes in the midst of the struggle, when the battle is almost unbearable, the circumstances look impossible, and He speaks peace to us and gives us the encouragement we need to boost our morale and keep us fighting. He is our peace, and that is the foundation upon which we must do battle. That is the relationship of the shoes to the rest of the armor.

The Requirement of the Shoes for Armor

Luke 21:26 tells us that in the last days men's hearts are going to be failing them for fear. Have you noticed how fear, stress and violence are increasing in our world? Men's hearts are starting to fail with fear, and because of that we are to be men and women who stand apart from the world; we are to have a ministry of peace to people who are afraid.

How can we minister to them if our own hearts are troubled and filled with fear? They will just look at us and wonder what we have to offer that is different. We must go into this world with a gospel message that brings peace and do it with the settled assurance that Jesus Christ is at home in our hearts, bringing peace to our souls.

The Reason for the Shoes as Armor

Matthew 6 tells us why we are to have peace. I often read this passage to people I visit in the hospital to remind them of His intimate concern and care for His own. It is in this passage that we are reminded that we don't have to be filled with anxiety or overrun with fear. It also reveals why, without God's peace operating in our lives, we will not win the spiritual battle. Let me suggest five reasons why we are not fit to go to war without the shoes of the gospel of peace.

Without Shoes, You Are Ungrateful

In Matthew 6:25 Jesus tells us, "Take no thought for your life, what ye shall eat, or what ye shall drink; nor for your body, what ye shall put on. Is not the life more than meat, and the body than raiment?" This last question is a rhetorical question. It is saying, "Don't be ungrateful for the provision you have." If you don't have the peace of God operating within your heart, you are ungrateful. You cannot be fighting fervently for the Lord and at the same time be doubting Him in the very basics of life. You cannot go into combat to be a warrior for the Lord Jesus while at the same time you are distrusting His very concern for you as His child. If you don't have on the shoes of the gospel of peace, you are ungrateful.

Without Shoes, You Are Unreasonable

Matthew 6:26 says, "Look at the birds of the air; for they neither sow nor reap, nor gather into barns; yet your heavenly Father feeds them." Then Jesus asks His audience, "Are you not of more value than they?" Jesus is saying, in essence, "Why worry about what is going on in your life? Look at the birds as an example. They don't know how to plant or harvest, but God always takes care of them because He loves them. Don't you think He loves you even more?" That's just not even reasonable to consider, is it? Surely God loves His children more than a flock of birds. To not wear the shoes of peace is unreasonable. It assumes that God doesn't really care, even though He has cared for you so many times in the past. Not to believe in the peace of Christ and not to practice that peace in your own life flies in the face of all logic.

Without Shoes, You Are Unproductive

If you choose to operate in the realm of worry, anxiety, and in the flesh, what are you going to accomplish? Matthew 6:27 says, "Which of you by worrying can add one cubit unto his stature?" My family has always been concerned about how tall everybody is. We have marks on our living room wall to measure height, and my son wants to grow to be 6'5". Now, he might want that in the worst way, but his desire and anxiety will do nothing to help him grow. You can't think your way to being 6'5". You can worry all you want, but it won't change things. Worry never changed anything, so what good is it? It is totally unproductive. If you do not have on the shoes of the gospel of peace you will accomplish nothing. Going through life on your own, taking care of circumstances, trying to fight the war without the peace of God, will lead you nowhere.

Without Shoes, You Are Unchristian

Take one more look at Matthew 6, verse 31: "Therefore do not worry, saying, 'What shall we eat?' or 'What shall we drink?' or 'Wherewithal shall we be clothed?' For after all these things the Gentiles seek." That word "Gentiles" is often translated "pagans," and the verse simply suggests that if you get all worked up with worry over how you will provide the basic necessities, you are acting no different than the world. There is nothing distinctly Christian about your attitudes.

The world worries over the question, "How can I get more?" But the Scriptures say if you spend your whole life spinning your wheels over temporal worries like that, you are not set apart from the world. Where is the sense of security and peace that is yours because you belong to Christ? Without the shoes of the gospel of peace, you are unchristian. Nobody can tell who you are; you look just like the world.

Without Shoes, Your Are Unprepared

"But seek first the kingdom of God and His righteousness, and all these things shall be added to you. Therefore do not worry about tomorrow, for tomorrow will worry about it's own things. Sufficient for the day is its own troubles" (Matthew 6:33-34). Jesus very clearly tells us in the Bible that our lives are to be filled with peace, not with worries over the things of this world. That's why

David wrote, "Cast your burden on the LORD, and He shall sustain you" (Psalm 55:22), and Peter said, "Casting all your care upon Him, for He cares for you" (1 Peter 5:7). You cannot be a warrior when you are torn up inside with doubt and worry. You cannot be strong and confident in battle, standing secure in Him, because you don't have the solid footing that comes with the shoes of the gospel of peace.

The Requisitioning of Shoes for Armor

If you were in the army and were without shoes, you would have to requisition them. So let me tell you how to requisition the shoes of the gospel of peace. First, you need to meet the Author of Peace. You may not have peace in your heart because you have never met the One who gives peace. Hebrews 13:20 calls Him "the God of peace." 2 Thessalonians 3:16 refers to Him as "the Lord of peace." 1 Corinthians 14:33 says, "For God is not the author of confusion, but of peace." He sent Christ into the world to be your savior and He wants you to come to know Him and fill up your life with His peace.

Second, you need to meditate on the Prince of Peace. Isaiah 26:3 tells us, "You will keep him in perfect peace, whose mind is stayed on You." As you meditate on the Author of Peace, He fills up your life with perfect peace.

Third, you need to manifest the spirit of peace in your life. The Bible says that peace is one of the inevitable results of the Spirit of God controlling your life. The fruit of the Spirit is love, joy, and peace. One way to tell if someone is controlled by the Spirit is by discerning a sense of quietness within their soul, even if all around them is turmoil.

We ought to pray every day, "Spirit of God, take control of my life. Cleanse me from sin. I confess it, and now, Spirit, take control. Take up residency in my heart. You sit on the throne of my life. I give myself totally to You." Then when bad thoughts return you bow your head and say, "Lord, I don't want it this way. I know it is a sin for me not to trust You. I confess my sin. Now Spirit of God, take control again and grant me peace." You might have to do that twenty times the first day. But as you learn how to give your life to the control of the Spirit of God, little by little He does get control and that sense of peace comes to reign within.

Fourth, we put on the shoes of the gospel of peace by meditating and memorizing the Word of peace. Psalm 119:165 tells us,

"Great peace have those who love your law." What a tremendous promise! If you meditate and memorize God's Word, then as you face the troubles and turmoils of battle, He will bring to mind the truth that you have committed to your heart and mind.

One of the reasons so many Christians are going down in battle is because they have nothing on which to rely when the fighting becomes difficult. They haven't filled their minds with the thoughts of God, so they have no thoughts with which to comfort and strengthen themselves. If you want to invest your time in something worthwhile, fill your heart and mind with the truth of God. Then when Satan attacks you can call forth God's Word to defeat him, and remain in perfect peace during the fiercest of battles. Jesus said in John 14:27, "Peace I leave with you, My peace I give to you; not as the world gives do I give to you. Let not your heart be troubled, and neither let it be afraid." And Jesus lived that out. You'll find it difficult to identify a time when Jesus was flustered, or in turmoil, or not at peace. The only time you see Him angry is when there is righteous anger against some evil being done. Even as Christ went to His death there was a calmness and sense of direction about the events. His life was secure, and He wants you to be standing firm, wearing the shoes of the gospel of peace.

APPLICATION

1. How many pairs of shoes do you have in your closet?

Where do you wear them? What special purposes do they serve?

Is it reasonable to think you could go to a formal dinner barefoot? Or to a construction site?

With that in mind, what important place do the shoes of the gospel of peace have in the armor?

2. Where do you see a lack of peace in the world?

What causes it?

Where do you see true peace?

Describe someone you know who seems totally at peace with himself/herself.

What three things most often disturb your inner peace?

What do you do to try to regain your peace?

3. Examine the following verses for principles of God's peace:

Psalm 29:11

Psalm 34:14

Psalm 55:22

Psalm 119:165

Proverbs 12:20

Mark 9:50

Romans 5:1

Romans 8:6

Romans 12:18

1 Corinthians 7:15

Galatians 5:22

Colossians 3:15

Hebrews 12:14

4. How is the gospel peace? (See Acts 10:36)

How has the gospel brought peace to your life?

Do you think people can see a change in your life because of the gospel?

How do you put Philippians 4:6-9 into practice in your life?

5. Re-write 1 Corinthians 14:33 in your own words.

How is God a God of peace?

What name is given to God in Romans 15:33, Philippians 4:9, 1 Thessalonians 5:23, and Hebrews 13:20?

What does Colossians 1:19-20 say that Christ did?

How do you reconcile those words with Christ's words in Matthew 10:34 and Luke 12:51?

6. What principle is taught in Ephesians 2:11-18?

How should that impact your Christian walk?

In your own words, what are we called to do in Ephesians 4:3?

7. What promise does Jesus make in John 14:27?

In the battle, do you feel the peace of God?

What steps could you take to ensure that your feet are shod with the shoes of the gospel of peace?

DID YOU KNOW

The Old Testament word for peace was "shalom," which literally means "completeness." In our modern day we tend to think of peace as the cessation of hostilities, but the Jewish mind considered peace to be a more inner, personal sense of well-being. That is why the prophet could write in Isaiah 32:17, "The work of righteousness will be peace. . . quietness and assurance forever." "Shalom" became the most common greeting in Jewish culture (hence all those New Testament introductions that begin with "Grace and peace to you"), and is still used today.

The Shield of Faith

Ephesians 6:16

OUTLINE

I n this lesson we will examine the shield and how to use it in our spiritual battle.

- I. The Priority of the Shield of Faith
- II. The Purpose of the Shield of Faith
- III. The Potential of the Shield of Faith
  - A. The Dart of Doubt
  - B. The Dart of Denial
  - C. The Dart of Deceit
- IV. The Possession of the Shield of Faith

OVERVIEW

When you study the history of the church, you discover that it was born in persecution, in martyrdom, in suffering, in imprisonment, and in bloodshed. Our Leader was executed and all of the apostles, with one exception, died a martyr's death. In the first centuries of the church it suffered unspeakable persecution. Foxe's Book of Martyrs tells the price that has been paid for our faith and the Bible tells us that that is normal for God's people. As a matter of fact, Scripture says that we aren't to think it strange when we face trouble; if we are going to reign with Christ we are going to suffer with Him (1 Peter 4:12-14). The true Christian experience is a spiritual war, and each of us must take up "the shield of faith with which you will be able to quench all the fiery darts of the wicked one" (Ephesians 6:16).

Satan's first work is to create doubt. That's what he did in the Garden of Eden, and he has been repeating his success in that area from those first days until our own day. He is always causing people to doubt God. The Bible says that the way we are to withstand this attack upon God and His promises is to take up the shield of faith. Once again, this is simply another way of expressing that we are to put on the Lord Jesus Christ and allow Him to be our defense. As Paul said in Galatians 2:20, "I have been crucified with Christ; it is no longer I who live, but Christ lives in me; and the life which I now live in the flesh I live by faith in the Son of God, who loved me and gave Himself for me." Even our faith is a gift from God—Jesus Christ, who is our shield.

The Priority of the Shield of Faith

The Bible says that as we go through life, we need to have a shield with us at all times because we are vulnerable. "Above all," Paul says, "take up the shield of faith." It is of primary importance. All the rest of the armor will be unable to fully protect you in battle if you are without your shield.

Do you remember Ahab, who went to do battle with the Assyrians? He was protected by body armor, which he disguised to keep from being recognized, and went to do battle. The Bible says that as the battle raged, a man took a bow and shot wildly into the air. That arrow entered the joints of Ahab's armor, pierced his side, and he bled to death inside his armor. He had armor, but no shield, so the arrow went between two pieces of armor and killed him.

Satan knows what armor we have and where the empty places are between the pieces of armor. Without the shield, which is wielded by the soldier and can be moved in any direction to deflect an attack, he is vulnerable. So the Bible says, "above all" do not forget your shield.

The Purpose of the Shield of Faith

Ephesians 6:16 tells us why we need the shield: "With it, you will be able to quench all the fiery darts of the wicked one." When the Scripture refers to fiery darts, it is a clear literary allusion to the practice of warfare at that time. Archers would soak the tips of their darts and arrows in poison, so that if the initial trauma of the arrow didn't kill its victim, the poison would get into the wound and do the job that way. On other occasions Roman soldiers would wrap their arrowheads in cloth, soak them in pitch, then set them on fire before raining arrows down on the enemy. Those flaming arrows splattered burning pitch wherever they landed, often setting afire the camp of the enemy. This proved particularly effective when fighting legions of soldiers with wooden shields, for those shields, while effectively stopping the arrow's thrust, would begin to burn. The smoke would make the shields difficult to use, and got in the eyes of the one wielding the shield. The Romans themselves had a habit of building shields made of wood, then covering them with animal skins and soaking them in water. When fiery darts came against them, the fire would be quenched and could not burn or destroy.

Christian, Satan knows exactly what he's doing when he shoots a dart into your life. Most of his darts are fire-tipped, and they have one purpose: to produce distress, depression, and disappointment in your life. Long after the initial thrust of the arrow is no longer felt, the sting of the fire can linger with you. The shield of faith can effectively stop, then extinguish, Satan's arrows, and help you to win the spiritual battle.

The Potential of the Shield of Faith

Perhaps you are thinking, "Sure, this pastor can talk about how Satan attacks, but he doesn't have any idea how hard it is for me personally. If he knew what I'm going through he wouldn't be writing so glibly about the shield of faith." That's the way many people feel, that nobody else can understand their particular problem. But does the Bible say, "so you will be able to quench most of Satan's fiery darts"? Does it promise, "You will find it quenches all the darts except the ones fired at you"? No, God's Word promises that if you hold fast to this truth it is sufficient to repel any attack Satan sends your way. Think about how the shield protects you.

The Dart of Doubt

What kinds of darts does Satan throw at you? In his first encounter with man, the devil used the dart of doubt. Genesis 3 records that he began to trap Eve by asking, "Has God indeed said, 'You shall not eat of every tree of the garden'?" In other words, did God really say that? Did God really mean it? He begins by creating a doubt in the mind of his victim. Satan shoots a dart into Eve's heart to question the integrity of God.

The Dart of Denial

When Eve replies, "We may eat the fruit of the trees of the garden; but of the fruit of the tree which is in the midst of the garden, God has said, 'You shall not eat it, nor shall you touch it, lest you die,'" Satan simply denies the truth. "You will not surely die," he says, though this is clearly a contradiction of God's Word. Notice that Satan didn't come right out at the beginning and deny God. That would have been too obvious and would have scared Eve off. He started by sowing seeds of doubt, then he brought it to a denial.

The Dart of Deceit

Satan sends his most poisonous dart into the heart of Eve when he says, "God knows that in the day you eat of it your eyes will be opened, and you will be like God, knowing good and evil." There is some truth in that statement, but it is full of wicked poison. It is a deceitful declaration, and Eve, without her shield of faith, was ruined by Satan's attack.

Satan still uses these darts to attack God's people. He loves to bring up doubt in the life of believers. That is why you use the shield of faith, which is the antithesis of doubt. In the book of Genesis you can read the account of Abram saving Lot. With 318 of his servants, Abram attacked the armies of the four kings who had captured Sodom, defeated them, and rescued his nephew and many others. Then he turned down a big reward. Later, as he pondered all that had taken place, Abram became afraid of retaliation.

Sometimes it is after our greatest victories that we begin to be afraid of failure and defeat. So in Genesis 15:1 the Lord says to Abram, "Do not be afraid, Abram. I am your shield, your exceedingly great reward." Satan tried to bring doubt into Abram's life, but God was a shield of faith protecting him.

Hebrews chapter 11 is called the "hall of faith," because it chronicles the people in the Old Testament who distinguished themselves by living expressions of faith. Each one accomplished great things by taking a step of faith, and it was that faith that protected them from the darts of the evil one. For example, consider the darts of doubt Noah must have had thrown at him: "Why are you building a boat, Noah? Out here? You really believe it will rain? It will take you forever to build this big boat!" You can be certain Satan tried to cast doubt about the reality of God's promise into Noah's mind.

Or consider the doubts Abram must have endured. "Don't you know where you are going, Abram? Why didn't God tell you? Wouldn't it be better to stop and think this through? How much can God care if He doesn't even tell you which way to go?" Years later, the devil must have tempted Abraham again by asking, "If God really loved you, and His promises are supposed to be fulfilled in Isaac, then why on earth are you going to go up the mountain to kill the boy? You must have misunderstood, Abraham. God couldn't have meant that."

The Bible is full of examples of men and women who held to their faith in God in the face of attacks from Satan. Sometimes people were called by God to do things that might have seemed ridiculous, but they stepped out in faith because they were sure God was directing them. Think what doubts Abraham's wife Sarah went through when the devil asked, "You're planning a nursery? At age ninety? Come on, Sarah, you are just too old!" Or the doubts thrown at the people of Israel as they walked around the walls of Jericho: "This is the stupidest military plan I've ever seen! You should be making up a plan of war, not simply marching around the walls and blowing trumpets." Don't you love Hebrews 11:30 when it says, "By faith the walls of Jericho fell down after they were encircled for seven days"? Can you imagine how much faith it took those people to keep doing what God told them to do, when in all of the outward appearance it made no sense? In our modern day we tend to think of those people as being zapped with some miraculous blast of faith that allowed them to stick it out, but I don't think that was the case. They felt many of the same pressures we feel, had the same doubts cast at them by Satan, and decided to lift up the shield of faith and say, "I'm going to believe God. He's given me a promise. I don't care what the circumstances look like, and I don't care what doubts Satan throws at me, this is God's Word and I will trust in it." Faith has the potential to accomplish great things for God.

The Possession of the Shield of Faith

God isn't going to one day drop this kind of faith in your lap. You have to take it up. You have to appropriate the truth. Faith is not faith unless it is at work. True faith is active, and the only way to appropriate it is to become familiar with the Word of God so that you know the truth and can fight off Satan's doubt and deceit with God's truth.

There are two things to keep in mind if you are going to pick up the shield of faith. First, get straight about the object of your faith— Jesus Christ. Don't just put your faith in a pastor or teacher, but in the One about whom they teach. As you get to know Christ, you will begin to feel more and more secure. Get to know Jesus and your faith will grow. Second, get serious about the strengthening of your faith. You develop physical strength by exercise, and you develop spiritual strength by exercising your faith. You don't grow by what you know, but by taking what you know and applying that truth to your life. If you don't exercise your faith by applying truth to your life, you won't grow. Do you want to build a strong shield of faith so that you can defeat Satan in the spiritual battle? Find something God has told you to do, and do it. Then you'll start to win some of those battles.

APPLICATION

1. When someone mentions a "person of great faith," who comes to your mind? Why?

What does a person of great faith have that you don't have?

How could you develop great faith?

2. What principles of faith do you glean from these passages:

Matthew 17:20

Mark 11:22-24

Romans 10:17

1 Corinthians 2:4-5

Galatians 2:20

Galatians 3:23-25

2 Thessalonians 1:3-4

1 Peter 1:6-7

3.Read Matthew 4:1-11. How did Satan try to deceive Jesus?

How did Jesus fight back?

How can you use that example in your life?

4. According to Romans 3:21-28, what place does faith play in our salvation? (see also Romans 4:4-5)

5. What does Paul have to say about the faith of others in Romans 14:1-4 & 22-23?

6. What do you think Habbakuk 2:4 means when it says, "the just shall live by his faith"?

7. Re-write 2 Corinthians 5:7 in your own words.

8. How do we put into practice 2 Corinthians 13:5?

9. Where do you have a tendency to doubt God?

Have you ever experienced a time of denial with God, only to realize your mistake later? What were the results of that time?

How do you see Satan trying to deceive the people around you?

10. Read through Hebrews 11. Which character stands out as a favorite pillar of faith?

What is it about his/her faith or actions that impress you?

What is the author's point in verse 39?

Summarize the message of Hebrews 11 in your own words.

11. Have you ever been called by God to do something bold, scary, or embarrassing? Tell about it.

Have you ever felt God calling you to do something and you said no?

How do you need to learn to trust God?

What could you do that would build your faith in the Lord?

DID YOU KNOW?

In Roman times there were two sorts of shields—large square ones that the front-line soldiers could hide behind as they advanced, and small ones that could be used to ward off blows in hand-to-hand combat. The soldiers at the front had to trust that their large wooden shields would hold up to the battering that assault troops always face and spent considerable time checking for cracks or weak spots in their shields. Those behind used both metal and wooden shields, and a skilled warrior learned to use his small shield as a battering weapon as much as a piece of defensive equipment.

The Helmet of Salvation

Ephesians 6:17

OUTLINE

In this lesson we will explore our salvation and the important part it plays in spiritual warfare.

I. **Picturing The Helmet of Salvation**
   A. It is Personified in Jesus Christ
   B. It is a Prerequisite to Any Kind of Ministry
   C. It is the Power of God in Your Life
   D. It is Produced by Reading the Word of God
   E. It is Possible Through Prayer

II. **Practicing The Helmet of Salvation**
   A. Defending Ourselves in a Hostile World
   B. Demolishing the Enemy's Stronghold in Our Minds

OVERVIEW

Awhile back, one of the men in our church gave me a letter describing an experience in his life that caused defeat, discouragement, and despair. It was his way of telling how Satan had won a victory, and how it felt. He said that he was given an invitation to a house that sounded like this: "Come on in, it's a great place to find friendship. It's exciting, the action is good, and the refreshments are excellent. We deceive a little, but we never get caught, so no one knows. And it's fun, so you can put off those pressures and responsibilities, relationships, and who God really is." So he walked into the door of that house. Inside he found amusements and excitement. He also found he didn't need to think. He could simply enjoy pleasure. Soon he was spending less time thinking and more time partying. He grabbed all he could to fill his empty life and stay busy. One day he realized he had experienced all the house had to offer and wanted to leave, but he could not. Even though it was a house of dead men, he had become a slave to that house.

Have you ever had an experience like that? Satan is in the business of waging a battle for the possession and control of your mind. His purpose is to corrupt or confuse you, whether through false teaching or the world's value system, so that it is impossible for you to think clearly about God and His purposes. That is why it is very important to examine the meaning behind Paul's statement that as believers we protect our minds with the helmet of salvation. Through Christ we can have victory in the area of the mind, where the devil fights many of his battles, since the Lord is our helmet. He is the girdle of truth, for He is the Way, the Truth, and the Life. He is the breastplate, for He is our righteousness. He becomes our shoes of peace, for He is our peace. He is the shield of faith, for He is the author and finisher of our faith. And He is the helmet of salvation, for we are told in the Bible that we have the mind of Christ.

Picturing the Helmet of Salvation

The helmet, which is the covering for our head, reminds us that Christ wants us to equip ourselves with His purposes, His plans, His thoughts, His concepts, His truth, and His revelation, so that we can stand victorious in the midst of the fury of Satan's attacks. I believe the spiritual battle is fought in the mental arena more than any other place in life. We love the Lord, but if we aren't careful the devil can enter our thinking process, set up an outpost, and begin to influence other areas of our life.

The helmet of salvation is more than simply knowing that we are Christians. When we put on the helmet we are literally equipping ourselves with the wisdom of God resident in the person of Jesus Christ. We are to take unto ourselves God's wisdom.

It is Personified in Jesus Christ

"But to those who are called, both Jews and Greeks, Christ the power of God and the wisdom of God. . . But of Him you are in Christ Jesus, who became for us wisdom from God—and righteousness and sanctification and redemption" (1 Corinthians 1:24, 30). Notice the progression in those thoughts. Not only are we saved by God's wisdom, we are also given God's wisdom. We are also made right with God and actually participate in His righteousness. On top of all that, we receive sanctification from God and He gives to us His great redemption. All of this is because of the person of Christ. As we encompass the Lord and "put on" Jesus Christ, He becomes to us our wisdom. The helmet is personified in Jesus Christ. He is our helmet of Salvation.

It is a Prerequisite to Any Kind of Ministry

My wife and I once rode motor scooters in the Dominican Republic. The streets were jammed with riders, and no one wears a helmet because they aren't required. I was told it isn't uncommon for there to be twenty or twenty-five motor scooter deaths in one day in Santa Domingo. Many would be prevented by wearing helmets.

When you go into spiritual battle as a minister of Jesus Christ, the helmet is not optional. You simply must wear it. You have to think like Christ. In the sixth chapter of Acts, when they were establishing the prerequisites for deacons, they decided, "Seek out from among you seven men of good reputation, full of the Holy Spirit and wisdom." Wisdom is a prerequisite to ministry. You must be wearing the helmet of salvation if you are going to be involved in serving Jesus Christ.

It is the Power of God in Your Life

If you don't have the helmet, you don't have power. Paul said in 1 Corinthians 2:3, "I was with you in weakness, in fear, and in much trembling. And my speech and my preaching were not with persuasive words of human wisdom, but in demonstration of the Spirit and of power, that your faith should not be in the wisdom of men but in the power of God." He did not go to the church at Corinth with his own concepts or his own program. He went equipped with the mind of God, and that gave him power.

It is Produced by Reading the Word of God

You gain God's wisdom through spending time with Him in His Word. That is why Paul could say to Timothy in 2 Timothy 3:15, "And that from childhood you have known the Holy Scriptures, which are able to make you wise for salvation." Young Timothy became wise by spending time in the Word. You are never going to have the wisdom of Christ if you don't invest some time reading the Bible. It won't come any other way. The Bible is God's message-His truth for us. It is the best way to come to know Him and know His mind.

It is Possible Through Prayer

How can you get the helmet of salvation? How can you gain the wisdom of God for your Christian life? You have to ask God for it. The Bible says in James 1:5, "If any of you lacks wisdom, let him ask of God, who gives to all liberally and without reproach, and it will be given to him." The helmet of salvation, which is the protection of the wisdom of God, is available to every believer. It is a prerequisite for anyone wanting to do ministry, and it is possible to obtain through prayer and the reading of the Word of God.

Practicing The Helmet of Salvation

The key to all this is knowing how to use the helmet of salvation. I grew up in a generation when it was thought to be almost a sign of spirituality to be ignorant. Many of the most influential churches rejected that fundamentalist notion and helped establish an intellectual basis for the Christian faith. The whole system of apologetics and education came as a result of the recognition that Christians were being sent out into the world ill-equipped in the mental arena to do battle with Satan. The power of ideas changes the world. It was the power of an idea that caused communism to be established, and the power of an idea that swept it out. The power of ideas empowered Hitler and Stalin, just as they empowered Luther and Augustine.

We have never been in a place where we more sorely needed men and women thoroughly equipped with Christian minds, ready to do battle in the spiritual arena. The battle is raging and we risk losing if we do not have champions for God that are determined to be every bit as equipped in the disciplines of the gospel as the greatest scientist is in his discipline.

Defending Ourselves in a Hostile World

The mind of Christ is not in accord with the mind of the world. Rather, it is in opposition to it. The world is hostile toward what you think and believe when you follow Christ. There is no place where that is more evident than in the early days of the church when the apostles went out to champion the cause of the gospel. Jesus promised in Matthew 10:18-20, "you will be brought before governors and kings for My sake, as a testimony to them and to the Gentiles. But when they deliver you up, do not worry about how or what you should speak. For it will be given to you in that hour what you should speak." That verse describes how the believer functions with the helmet of salvation in place. Jesus said that there will be times in your Christian life when you will be caught in a hostile situation, with no time to prepare. You won't have an opportunity to pull out your apologetics text, so you will trust the Lord because you have equipped yourself with the mind of Christ. In that moment, as you are being attacked by enemy forces, you don't have to worry because God will give you the right words to say.

There are illustrations of that throughout the book of Acts. The young apostles, equipped with the Holy Spirit and empowered with the resurrection power, had something about their speech and lives that caught the attention of the world. For instance, Peter was defending himself before the Sanhedrin, and that counsel marveled at his words although he was an unlearned, ignorant man. Peter spoke with an authority that was a part of the wisdom of God operating in his life. Acts 5:33 tells us, "When they heard this, they were furious and plotted to kill them." Here is a common fisherman speaking to the intelligentsia with such power that it gripped their hearts with fear—so much fear that the only way they knew how to deal with him was to kill him.

Later in Acts, Paul confronted the Jews at Damascus, proving that Jesus is the Christ. He also debated the Sanhedrin in Jerusalem, defended himself before a raging mobs, and argued before Felix, Festus, and King Agrippa, each time giving the gospel message and recounting his own conversion. His life evidenced one truth: there was something in his communication that was beyond natural ability. He had the power of God in his life and he was equipped with the helmet of salvation. Men and women today need to be so equipped. We cannot walk into the world without any answers. Too many Christians spend their lives on the defensive, running away from confrontation, because they have not equipped themselves with the mind of Christ. We need believers who can embrace His truth and boldly communicate it to a lost world.

Demolishing the Enemy's Stronghold in Our Minds

The other place where we can use the helmet of salvation is in the inner battle with our sin nature. 2 Corinthians 10:4-6 says, "For the weapons of our warfare are not carnal but mighty in God for pulling down strongholds, casting down arguments and every high thing that exalts itself against the knowledge of God, bringing every thought into captivity to the obedience of Christ." The word translated "strongholds" is an old military term for "fortress," and it refers to a place where the enemy is entrenched. Satan operates in the area of the mind, setting up a beachhead and then fanning out to conquer your life. With some it is an openness to lewd pictures, which develops into a problem with pornography, which eventually can totally defeat the individual. But the Bible says that it is the power of the believer to be able to break those strongholds, raze the fortresses and recapture the territory of our minds for Christ Jesus. It won't happen right away, and it won't come easy, but it can be done through the power of God. To do so you must get into God's Word, study those passages that relate to the strongholds Satan has in your life, and let the mind of Christ begin to give you victory over it.

Sometimes I get the impression Christians think the Bible is a magic book—"a chapter a day keeps the devil away." But you can't put God's Word on your nightstand, look at it affectionately before you go to bed at night, pat it when you get up in the morning, and expect it to change your life. That's not how it works. If His Word is going to change you, if His thoughts are going to be your thoughts, then you have to study your Bible, master its truth, and commit it to your mind and heart so that it can begin to assault those strongholds in your life.

APPLICATION

1. In your own words, what does it mean to have the mind of Christ?

Why is that important?

What good will it do you?

Why is it necessary to have the mind of Christ before getting into a ministry?

2. What principles regarding the helmet of salvation can you glean from the following passages of Scripture?

Matthew 16:23

Luke 10:27

Romans 7:22-23

Romans 8:6-7

Romans 11:33-34

Romans 12:1-2

Philippians 4:8

Colossians 3:2

Titus 1:15

3. What does 1 Corinthians 2:11-16 teach us about having the mind of Christ?

Take a look at Ephesians 2:1-5 and 4:17-24. How are our Christian minds to be different from those of non-Christians?

How can a Christian "renew" his or her mind, as mentioned in Romans 12?

4. Do you see the world as hostile to your Christian message?

Is that good or bad?

Have you ever had to defend your faith in a hostile environment?

What did you say? How was it received?

What possible situations could arise where you would again have to take a committed stand for Christ in the face of hostility?

What could you do to prepare for the eventuality?

How do you think Paul, Peter, and the other apostles were able to make such an impact on their world for the cause of Christ?

How could they have known what to say?

Is there anything we can learn from their example?

5. How can the Bible change your life?

6. What do the following verses have to say about the use of Scripture in the life of the Christian:

Romans 10:17

Colossians 3:16-17

2 Timothy 2:15

2 Timothy 3:16-17

Hebrews 4:12

1 Peter 1:23-25

1 Peter 2:2

2 Peter 1:19-21

1 John 2:14

7. Re-write James 1:22-25 in your own words.

8. In your view, how does Satan set up strongholds?

What strongholds has Satan set up in your life?

.vno could you trust to talk with about breaking them down?

What could you do to begin to break down Satan's fortresses?

DID YOU KNOW?

Most helmets worn by Roman soldiers were not the fancy kind with ostrich feathers that you've come to love on Ben Hur. The helmets were hammered out of metal, all the same size, and were designed more to ward off blows than to march in a parade. They required leather or linen stuffing on the inside to make them fit properly, and often had a chinstrap to keep them from falling or getting twisted during battle (a common complaint of Roman soldiers). It took quite a bit of money to get a fancy helmet custom made to fit your head, so only the high-ranking officers and political generals had those. Most were simple shells, the thicker the better, because they took a beating in nearly every battle, and they could get extremely hot and uncomfortable. The Roman armies considered helmets their most significant piece of armor, and had severe penalties for anyone caught without one.

The Sword
of the Spirit

Ephesians 6:17

OUTLINE

In this lesson we will examine the sword of the Spirit and how we can use it in battle.

I. The Explanation of the Sword of the Spirit
II. The Effect of the Sword of the Spirit
    A. The Illustration of Jesus
    B. The Example of the Christian Life

OVERVIEW

All of the armor we have looked at so far has been defensive armor. It is given to ward off the attacks which come from the evil one. But the Lord has also given us an offensive weapon: the sword of the Spirit, which is the Word of God. Every warrior needs a weapon for offensive warfare, and the weapon God has chosen is His Word, the Bible. Actually, it is that which we take from the Bible that we use as our sword.

The Explanation of the Sword of the Spirit

There are two Greek words which are translated in the Scripture as the term "word." The first, *logos*, is the most common. That is the term found in John chapter 1 when it refers to Jesus Christ as the Word. But that is not the word we find in Ephesians 6:17. Instead, Paul used the Greek word *rhema*, and it is essential to discover the difference if we are to understand and arm ourselves with the sword of the Spirit. The *rhema* of God literally means "the sayings of God," and it refers to the fact that God has available wisdom for your specific situations. In other words, the Bible is like an armory, and inside are all sorts of swords that you can pull out when you need to attack the enemy.

In Romans 10:17 the word *rhema* is also used: "So then faith comes by hearing, and hearing by the *rhema* of God." Now I always thought that verse meant that if you read the Bible, you will get faith. But later I discovered that it means: As you read God's Word, He will pull out sayings that just become alive and touch your heart. When you experience that, your faith becomes alive. Maybe you have had an experience where a verse of Scripture just came alive and spoke to your need of the moment. It became yours like never before. The *rhema*, or saying of God, became a revelation for you. That is the same sense Paul was getting at in Ephesians 6.

Now you can see why it is essential for Christians to understand this passage. Too many believers act like the Bible is a lucky rabbit's foot, and their success in the spiritual war is simply to carry a Bible under their arm. But you aren't fit to fight unless you can pull out the *rhema*, the sayings of God that are appropriate and effective for the need at hand.

The Effect of the Sword of the Spirit

Hebrews 4:12 says, "For the word of God is living and powerful, and sharper than any two-edged sword, piercing even to the division of soul and spirit, and of joints and marrow, and is a discerner of the thoughts and intents of the heart." That passage is militant about the Bible. It says the Scripture is alive, powerful, and can pierce the heart of men, even causing an enemy to retreat. It is useful for discerning truth, and it is the most dreaded weapon we can use against the enemy. A metal sword may pierce the body, but the Word of God pierces the heart. A metal sword gets dull as you use it, but the sword of the Spirit is sharpened with use. A metal sword requires the practiced hand of the soldier to be effective, but the sword of the Spirit requires nothing. It carries its own power, and is able to function apart from the soldier's hand. A metal sword wounds to hurt, but the sword of the Spirit wounds to heal.

Consider how effective it is. Peter preached on the day of Pentecost in Acts 2:37 and the sword worked wonders. "Now when they heard this, they were cut to the heart, and said to Peter and the rest of the apostles, 'Men and brethren, what shall we do?'" The sword was turned loose that day by Peter and he preached the Word of God concerning sin and judgment and the resurrection of Jesus Christ. The sword pierced the hearts of the people who listened in such a way that the Scripture says they gave the invitation instead of the preacher! They asked, "What are we to do?"

Another illustration is in Acts 5:33. Here again the apostles and Peter have been talking and we read that "when they heard this, they were furious, and plotted to kill them." The sword of the Spirit, unleashed, has the power to cut right into the heart of a person. Sometimes they respond with anger to the truth. Have you ever experienced the Word of God like that? Have you ever heard a sermon and known that every word was directed right at your heart? That's the sword of the Spirit at work.

The Illustration of Jesus

Christ is the master swordsman when it comes to using this weapon. In Matthew 4:1-11 we read about the temptation of Jesus in the wilderness that took place right after His baptism. At the end of chapter 3 God has said, "This is my beloved Son, in whom

I am well pleased." Right after that the Spirit leads Him into the wilderness where Satan tempts Him to question what God said about Jesus at the baptism. There are three temptations that are all along the same lines he has used since the beginning of history. He always uses the same old temptations, "the lust of the flesh, the lust of the eyes, and the pride of life" (1 John 2:16). It's the same way he tempted Eve. He said the fruit was good for food (the lust of the flesh); he said the fruit was pleasant to the eyes (the lust of the eyes); and he claimed it was able to make one wise (the pride of life). He never changes.

When we examine the temptation recorded in Matthew 4, we find he uses exactly the same temptations. First there was the lust of the flesh: "And Jesus was led up by Spirit into the wilderness to be tempted by the devil. And when He had fasted forty days and forty nights, afterward He was hungry. Now when the tempter came to Him, he said, 'If you are the Son of God, command that these stones become bread.'" The problem with this temptation is obvious when you examine it. Satan is simply saying, "Satisfy your hunger by turning the stones into bread. Just do a little miracle." But the idea behind it is insidious. "If you are really God, why are you hungry? Use your super-human power to meet your human needs." Had Christ succumbed to that, He would have ceased at that moment to function as a man. His incarnation would have been aborted. Satan was trying to destroy His mission on earth by getting Jesus to act independently of the Father. He wanted to use the human hunger Christ felt to trick Him into satisfying His own need. Never in all of Scripture does Jesus do a miracle for Himself. He said, "the Son of Man did not come to be served, but to give His life a ransom for many" (Matthew 20:28). His whole purpose in life was to minister to others. Satan tried to get Him to do a miracle for Himself.

Faced with that temptation, Jesus reached into His sheath and pulled out a sword: "But He answered and said, 'It is written, Man shall not live by bread alone, but by every word that proceeds from the mouth of God'" (Deuteronomy 8:3). God keeps people alive, not bread. The Heavenly Father could bring nourishment, and He wouldn't need bread to do it. It's interesting that the key word in Christ's response is "alone." In other words, man shall not live apart from the will of God. He is to walk in dependence upon God. Jesus was telling Satan that He would not walk independently of His father. The Bible tells us to walk according to the will of God, and that's what Jesus had determined to do. Jesus beat back the devil with the sword of the Spirit, the Scripture.

Temptation number two was the lust of the eyes: "Then the devil took Him up into the holy city, set Him on the pinnacle of the temple, and said to Him, 'If You are the Son of God, throw Yourself down. For it is written: 'He shall give His angels charge over you,' and 'In their hands they shall bear You up, lest you dash your foot against a stone.'" This temptation took place 450 feet above the Kidron Valley, high on the wall of the temple. The rabbis had a tradition that the Messiah would land on the temple roof, so if Jesus had jumped off the pinnacle He would certainly have been identified as the Messiah. Satan was trying to eliminate the problem of the first temptation by getting the Father to do a miracle for Jesus. He also quoted the Bible, although he did so inaccurately, leaving out the phrase from Psalm 91:12, "For He shall. . . keep you in all your ways." He perverted the text by leaving out that part of the passage that would remind Jesus that His Heavenly Father was in control and would take care of Him no matter what. The devil is very shrewd. You see, in the first temptation, Satan was trying to get Christ to distrust His Father and act independently. In the second temptation he was trying to get Christ to trust God more than He should, to be presumptuous and jump from the roof so that His Father would catch Him. The devil wanted Christ to set Himself up as a wonder-worker, to put on a show and win a large following. But the Lord had His sword ready and, reaching in, came out with, "It is written again, You shall not tempt the LORD your God" (Deuteronomy 6:16). God is not our servant to be ordered around. Christ was not going to be presumptuous with God. It is absolutely right to believe in miracles; it is absolutely wrong to try to schedule them.

Temptation number three was the pride of life. "Again the devil took Jesus up on an exceedingly high mountain, and showed Him all the kingdoms of the world and their glory. And he said to Him, 'All these things I will give You if You will fall down and worship me.'" He used his power to appeal to the Lord's personal ambition. Satan was telling Jesus that the end justifies the means. He was encouraging the Lord to take a shortcut to His goal. After all, Jesus came to set up a kingdom, so Satan offers an immediate, physical kingdom in place of the spiritual kingdom. "Forget about death, sacrifice, and salvation," the devil suggests. "Why suffer? You can gain your kingdom without the cross." Once more Jesus reached into the sheath of swords and pulled out the right one: "It is written, 'You shall worship the LORD your God, and Him only you shall serve'" (Deuteronomy 6:13).

And do you know what happened? Verse 11 tells us, "Then the devil left Him." Jesus won! He used the sword of the Spirit, which is the Word of God. He used the *rhema*, the sayings of God which He knew were appropriate. James, the brother of Jesus, tells us if we resist the devil, he will flee from us. You resist the devil with the sayings of God.

The Example of the Christian Life

Does this truth explain the dynamic of preaching to you? Perhaps you've gone to church with a need, heard a sermon on something else entirely, and God used a verse of Scripture or a story like a sword, piercing your heart and touching you on a subject that is totally different than the point of the message. I am always overwhelmed when someone gives their heart to Christ after a sermon aimed entirely at people who are already Christians! A Bible preacher slings arrows out in every direction. Some are going to pierce hearts with the *rhema* of God and because of that people will walk away changed. The Word of God impacts lives.

The sword of the Spirit also explains the discipline of reading your Bible systematically. Many Christians only want to read the gospels, or will never stray from the letters of Paul. Many believers today complain about the Old Testament books—too old, too harsh, too complex. Yet where did Jesus get all three of His swords? He got them all from the book of Deuteronomy. If you don't go through the entire Bible, you'll miss a lot of good swords.

Finally, the sword of the Spirit exhorts us to memorize key passages of God's Word. Can you see the Lord Jesus in the wilderness saying, "Hold on a minute, Satan, I have to get my concordance"? Yet many Christians go into battle like that. You know, most temptations in my life don't come while I have a Bible in my hands. They come when there is no Bible around. So I need to store up those swords in my mind, so that when temptation comes I can call them forth to use them in warding off the attack of Satan. That's what Paul meant when he said, "Let the word of Christ dwell in you richly." The psalmist also writes, "Your word I have hidden in my heart, that I might not sin against You"(Psalm 119:11). Be filled with God's truth so that when temptation comes you will know how to deal with it. If you don't get a grip on your Bible, you don't have a sword, and that means you are walking into battle unarmed.

APPLICATION

1. In what ways is the sword of the Spirit an offensive weapon?

In what ways is it a defensive weapon?

2. Read Matthew 4:1-11. To what human desires does Satan appeal in each of the three temptations of Christ?

How has Satan used these desires to tempt you?

When are you most vulnerable to those temptations?

What does Jesus do to resist each temptation?

How could you imitate the example of Christ in a temptation you are facing?

What does this passage reveal about our enemy?

3. What does Psalm 1 reveal about a person who spends time in God's Word?

In your own words, summarize the meaning of Hebrews 4:12-13.

What principles for using the sword of the Spirit do you learn from Psalm 19:7-11?

Read through Psalm 119, noting verses that reflect using the Word of God as the sword of the Spirit.

4. Have you ever presumed upon God? What happened?

Have you ever given God a "time limit" or decided to "sin now and ask forgiveness later"?

Why is that wrong?

When do you find it difficult to be dependent on God?

What promise does Paul make in 1 Corinthians 10:12-13?

5. Read Genesis chapter 39. Does Joseph bear any responsibility for what happened?

How did Satan use Joseph's strengths to set him up for this temptation?

Why does Joseph refuse to sin?

What rationalization could he have used?

Have you ever been surprised by temptation in a situation where you felt secure?

Do your feelings of responsibility help you resist temptation?

Have you ever felt you had to literally run away from temptation?

What was the cost to Joseph? Do you think Joseph regretted his response?

What would his cost have been had he given in?

6. What must we do to arm ourselves with the sword of the Spirit?

How would you like to be armed?

What steps might you take to stand more firmly against your opponents in the spiritual battle?

Praying Always with All Prayer

Ephesians 6:18

OUTLINE

I n this lesson we will look at the prayer life of a warrior.

   I. The Persistence of the Warrior's Prayer
  II. The Possibilities of the Warrior's Prayer
 III. The Petition of the Warrior's Prayer
 IV. The Power of the Warrior's Prayer
  V. The Precision of the Warrior's Prayer
 VI. The Perseverance of the Warrior's Prayer
VII. The Purpose of the Warrior's Prayer

OUTLINE

I once borrowed a car, and as a favor to the owner filled it with gas. That big Oldsmobile station wagon had an ornament on the hood that said "diesel," a sticker on the rear gate that said "Oldsmobile Diesel," and a note on the fuel gauge reading, "Diesel Fuel Only." So naturally I put diesel fuel in the tank. Big mistake, since the owner had recently converted it to gasoline. When it broke down on the main street of a village in New York, I had to explain to everyone in town why I had put diesel fuel into a vehicle with a gasoline engine.

I don't think I'll ever live that down, so I use it as the perfect illustration of Christians. We are human beings, and we have "Human Being" written all over us, but we've been converted into something else. We don't use the same sort of fuel we used to; we need a high octane spiritual fuel now. If you try to run your new spiritual self on the old kind of fuel, it won't work. There are a lot of Christians who haven't figured that out yet, and they spend their time wondering why they can't get their spiritual life running smoothly. The fuel for the Christian life, according to Ephesians 6:18, is prayer. Prayer is the energy that makes it possible for the Christian warrior to wear the armor and wield the sword.

Praying Always With All Prayer

You cannot fight the battle in your own power. No matter how talented you are, if you try to fight the spiritual battle in your own strength you will be defeated. Like the Oldsmobile, you will sputter, choke, stop, and have no power. You simply must be in contact with the One who gives power to His soldiers. Every warrior must keep in constant contact with his Commander through the ministry of prayer.

Throughout Scripture there are illustrations of the power of prayer in battle. Moses prayed on the mountain and God gave Joshua the victory over the Amalekites. Joshua prayed and the walls of Jericho fell before him. Gideon prayed and his 300 soldiers routed the Midianite hordes. As you study the Old Testament you will see that when Israel fought in her own strength, she was defeated. But when she cast herself upon the Lord and trusted in His might, victory always followed. King Hezekiah, after conquering the Assyrians, said in 2 Chronicles

32:8, "With us is the LORD our God, to help us and to fight our battles." The Lord is with us, fighting. That is the message of Ephesians 6:18.

The Persistence of the Warrior's Prayer

Notice how many times the word "all" occurs in this passage: "Praying always with all prayer and supplication in the Spirit, being watchful to this end with all perseverance and supplication for all the saints." The verse takes a comprehensive view of the ministry of prayer, just as Paul did when he said, "Pray without ceasing." Praying always doesn't mean we go around muttering under our breath, but that we keep a constant attitude of trust and communication with God at every moment. You are always to be available to God, and He to you.

Satan will use every device to keep you from praying. He will cause fatigue, doubt, discouragement, and depression to seep into your life so as to keep you from your true source of power. That is why you need to be praying regularly, not just when you feel like it. The enemy wants to keep you out of touch with God and occupied with other matters. But you must be constantly in prayer because, as a soldier, you are constantly in danger.

The Possibilities of the Warrior's Prayer

What does it mean to be "praying always with all prayer"? First, it means that we are to pray on all occasions. You can pray in public worship, in prayer groups, and in private. Second, it means that we are to pray in all places. We should be praying in the car, in the classroom, in the office, and around the family table. We are to pray in both prosperity and adversity. We are to pray morning, noon, and night. Third, we are to pray for all things. Pray for personal needs, family needs, business needs, and church needs. All things should be bathed in prayer. It ought to be possible, at any time and without long preparation, for you to get in touch with God. Prayer, talking with God, should come as naturally as breathing: "Lord, show me what to do." "Father, help me to understand your will at this moment." The possibilities for prayer are endless. We can pray on all occasions, in every place, at all times, for all things.

The Petition of the Warrior's Prayer

"Praying always with all prayer and with supplication." The word "supplication" simply means "to ask." Ask God for what you need. Of course you are to come in worship, thanksgiving, and gratitude, but you must also come asking. The Bible says we have not because we ask not (James 4:2). It is sometimes surprising to see how easy it is for us to go on striving for that which we have not yet asked. We ask in prayer because that is the only way God is going to work on our behalf.

Charles Hadden Spurgeon, the great British preacher, once said, "Asking is the rule of the kingdom. It is a rule that will never be altered... God will bless Elijah and send rain, but Elijah must pray for it. God will deliver the Jews, but Daniel must pray for it." When the Bible tells us that we are to pray always with all prayer and supplication, it means that the things we have need of we are to ask God for. We are to come and, in supplication, beseech Him. That's why we keep prayer lists. Too many Christians spend their energy worrying about things, when they could be praying to God about them.

Asking is the rule of the kingdom, and God has the resources to meet your need. Can you imagine your child coming to you, asking for something they know you can provide and that will be good for them, and you denying their request? Of course not! You provide it because you love them. But if your child does not ask, you cannot supply. God already knows what you need and He has put in place a channel for you to approach Him and ask. If we have not, it is because we have not asked.

The Power of the Warrior's Prayer

"Praying always with all prayer and supplication in the Spirit." The power of your prayer is the power of the Holy Spirit who lives in you. He determines not only the character but the content of your prayer. Have you ever wondered if what you pray is the will of God? Well, the Spirit, who wrote God's Word and lives in you, will direct you to the things of God as you submit to Him. Romans 8:26-27 says that it is only through the Spirit's power that we can pray in the will of God. Otherwise you are praying in your own power. As you are controlled by the Holy Spirit, His power is available to you in prayer.

As you spend time with God, through prayer and Bible reading, the Spirit makes clear what God's will is. You come into agreement with it, pray in the Spirit's power, and you will see mighty things happen. There is power in a warrior's prayer.

The Precision of the Warrior's Prayer

"Being watchful to this end. . ." The warrior must be watchful of his prayer life. In other words, he must diligently pray and be vigilant, permitting nothing in his life to disrupt his prayer life. Prayer is not just that which is confined to the moments you are on your knees. Prayer begins hours before, in the decisions you make. He guards his time, plans his schedule, watches for everything that feeds his prayer life, and guards against everything that hinders it. That is what it means to be watchful.

Jesus commands us to watch and pray. In Mark 13:33 He says, "Take heed, watch and pray." In Mark 14:38 He put it, "Watch and pray, lest you enter into temptation." Do you remember how Nehemiah defeated the enemy by watching and praying? In Nehemiah 4:9 it states, "We made our prayer to our God, and. . . we set a watch."

That word, "watch," is the Greek word which literally means "to be awake." It was used by the military to warn sentries of their duty. They were to stay awake when watching the gate, to make sure the enemy didn't sneak in and attack them. Here it means to be on the alert spiritually, staying awake in prayer, vigilant for the enemy's attacks. Peter went to sleep when he was supposed to watch and pray and he ended up getting into trouble. That is one of the reasons I often walk and pray, because it keeps me alert and focused while I speak with God. Many believers find their minds wandering during prayer, but that's the same as wandering away from a friend in the middle of a conversation. Colossians 4:2 says, "Continue earnestly in prayer, being vigilant in it with thanksgiving." In other words, be alert when you pray, like a soldier guarding the gate.

The Perseverance of a Warrior's Prayer

"Being watchful to this end with all perseverance." We need to continue praying, for when you stop praying you are headed for trouble. Romans 12:12 puts it, "Rejoicing in hope, patient in tribulation, continuing steadfastly in prayer." When it comes to praying, we need to hold on, not quiting or yielding to discouragement, and not being distracted by outside pressures. Prayer is never going to be something we just automatically do. Prayer is a matter of personal discipline. We have to take time to be holy. We have to exercise ourselves unto godliness. No matter what it takes, we must persevere in prayer or we will fall out of communication with our

Commander and become a casualty of war.

You might be discouraged about your prayer life. Satan likes to convince you that you've blown it and should no longer pray. He likes to get you to cancel your prayer time due to outside pressures. But we must learn to persevere. If you've never been a prayer warrior, start today. Prayer is crucial for your survival and success on the battlefield.

The Purpose of the Warrior's Prayer

"Praying always. . . for all the saints and for me." The purpose of your praying is that you might pray for others. Did you know that the word translated "saints" in the Bible is always plural? It is never found in the singular. We are to pray for each other, corporately. Perhaps that is why the Lord's prayer begins "Our Father," and not "My Father." We are not going into battle alone, but as part of God's army, and we are to uphold one another in prayer.

If you study the prayers of Paul in Scripture, you'll find he always prayed for his friends. There are examples of Paul praying and asking God to grant his friends wisdom, power, love, comfort, and the knowledge of God's will. Do you pray like that for your friends? Or do you simply pray for them to "have a nice day"? We ought to pray like warriors, and ask God to grant each other power and strength and wisdom. Perhaps we need to begin asking the Lord to help each believer put on the armor of God so that we will be ready for the battle with the evil one.

The Christian is built to run on prayer. If he doesn't pray, he won't run. You can try putting anything you want into the engine of your life, but if you are a Christian, the only thing that will work is prayer.

APPLICATION

1. What specific instructions are given in Ephesians 6:18 on how to pray?

Which of those instructions would you highlight as the one you most need to work on?

Why is prayer so important to Christian warriors?

How did Paul want the Ephesians to pray for him in verses 19 and 20?

Why do you think he asked for that kind of prayer?

Write out a short prayer that would have been appropriate for Paul.

2. What's the main obstacle that keeps you from praying?

Do you know a prayer warrior? Describe him/her.

3. What principles for praying can you take from the following verses:

Matthew 14:23

Matthew 19:13

Mark 11:24

Luke 6:12

Luke 22:39-46

Acts 1:14 & 2:42

Romans 8:26

Romans 12:12

Philippians 1:3-4

Colossians 4:2

1 Thessalonians 5:17

2 Thessalonians 3:1

1 Timothy 2:8

Hebrews 13:18-19

James 5:13-16

4. How would you define prayer?

How do we develop power in prayer?

What role does the Holy Spirit play in prayer?

If God already knows what we need, why bother praying?

Tell about an answer to prayer that you have experienced.

5. Read Matthew 6:5-13. What does Jesus warn us about?

How does He command us to pray?

What are the essential elements of the Lord's prayer?

Is there a model to follow in the Lord's prayer?

6. What does Paul request for others in each of the following passages:

Ephesians 1:18-19

Ephesians 3:16-19

Philippians 1:9-11

Colossians 1:9

1 Thessalonians 3:9-13

2 Thessalonians 1:11-12

2 Thessalonians 2:16-17

2 Thessalonians 3:5

1 Timothy 2:1-2

Philemon 6

What do these reveal about how we ought to pray for others?

Paul had something he prayed about for years, but God didn't resolve it. In 2 Corinthians 12:7-9, Paul reveals that he had a "thorn in the flesh," some trouble that he repeatedly asked God to remove. Instead, Paul was given the grace to live with it—so his desire was granted, although his request was not. Christians often struggle with the problem of unanswered prayer, but God's Word is quite clear. He will not grant our requests if we have sin in our hearts (Psalm 66:18), lack faith (Hebrews 11:6), ask with the wrong motive (James 4:3), or are asking as a show of pride (Luke 18:11-14). But He has promised to answer our requests when we abide in Christ, ask in His name, and pray in the Spirit. Still, sometimes for sound reasons that only He knows, He does not grant every request. The Christian's response is to trust Him.

The Real Holy War

Galatians 5:16-26

OUTLINE

This lesson will explore how we gain victory over Satan.

I. **The Inner War**
   A. The Flesh is Weak
   B. The Flesh is Worthless
   C. The Flesh is Warring
   D. The Flesh is Without Righteousness
   E. The Flesh is Wounded Mortally
II. **Winning the Inner War**
   A. Crucify the Flesh
   B. Walk in the Spirit

OUTLINE

The armor of God protects the believer from Satan's every attack. However, as you study the Bible it becomes clear that we have more than one enemy. John speaks of three adversaries that plague Christians: the world, the flesh, and the devil. Satan brings individual attacks, but the flesh attacks us through our internal desires and the world through external influences. Each area needs a unique strategy. In order to gain victory over the devil, you have to put on the armor, fight the war, and resist him. To gain victory over the flesh, you have to learn what it means to walk in the Spirit. To gain victory over the world, you must have faith in Jesus Christ who has already overcome the world. To put it another way, to be victorious over Satan, you have to fight; to be victorious over the flesh, you have to flee; to be victorious over the world, you have to forsake its influence by faith.

The Inner War

There is an inner war that goes on inside every one of us, a war between the flesh and the Spirit. Galatians 5:17 says it this way: "The flesh lusts against the Spirit, and the Spirit against the flesh; and these are contrary to one another, so that you do not do the things that you wish." In order to understand this concept, keep in mind that the word "flesh" in the Bible is used two separate ways. It is used as a synonym for the body, to describe the humanity of man. In John 3:6 we read, "That which is born of flesh is flesh, and that which is born of the Spirit is spirit." There is nothing evil in this at all, it is simply a descriptive term for the human body. Yet when the old and new nature each want to use the body for their own advantage, there is conflict—and that leads us to the other definition.

The second use of the term "flesh" has more of a theological flavor. Scripture says that man apart from God is flesh. When the word is used this way it is always in an evil sense. It speaks of the earthly nature of man apart from divine influence, and therefore it is a nature prone to sin and opposed to God. It is this flesh which frequently debases the body and uses it for sin. Because of the old nature there is an avenue whereby Satan can approach us with temptation. The flesh, the old nature, provides Satan with opportunities for attack. We are in the flesh, all of us, until we become

Christians. Then we receive the Spirit of God and are transformed by His power. We are only fleshly people until we meet Christ and our spiritual nature is made alive.

The Flesh is Weak

Romans 6:19 warns us that the flesh is weak. It doesn't have any strength to merit God's favor. So when God gave the Law to man, he could not maintain it. Man could not attain holiness by perfectly obeying rules. Why? Because the flesh is weak. That's the reason Christ had to come to bring grace, because there wasn't a man who had enough strength or ability or fortitude to live up to the high standards of the law. The flesh is too weak and we all sin.

Someone has written:

> Run and do the Law demands,
> yet gives me neither feet nor hands.
> But better news the gospel brings.
> It bids me fly and gives me wings.

The Flesh is Worthless

Paul says in Romans 7:18, "For I know that in me (that is, in my flesh) nothing good dwells." He acknowledged that there is nothing good in his flesh apart from God, an idea that flies in the face of all the humanistic thinking in our culture today. We are told that we can improve the flesh, make it better until ultimately it will be perfect. Yet John 6:63 tells us, "the flesh profits nothing." It is worthless.

The Flesh is Warring

Romans 8:7 reads, "The carnal (fleshly) mind is enmity against God." The flesh is weak and cannot hold the law, it is worthless and cannot help us, and it is at war with God and His Holy Spirit. There is a war going on inside each of us; a war that is between the old man and the new man. The old man is without hope and dead to God, but the new man has eternal hope and has been made alive in Christ Jesus. "The flesh lusts against the Spirit," Paul wrote in Galatians 5:17. All of us struggle with this inner battle.

The Flesh is Without Righteousness

Try as we may, the flesh doesn't have the ability to produce righteousness in a Christian's life. A person who lives in the flesh cannot please God and it is futile to try. "Are you so foolish?" Paul asks in Galatians 3:3. "Having begun in the Spirit, are you now being made perfect in the flesh?" He was writing to a church who thought that once Jesus had saved them, they could add to His work by fulfilling the old Jewish Law. Paul told them in essence, "You can't do anything by your works to make yourself perfect, since the flesh is without ability to produce righteousness."

The Flesh is Wounded Mortally

"Knowing this, that our old man was crucified with Him, that the body of sin might be done away with, that we should no longer be slaves of sin" (Romans 6:6). The flesh, which is the old man, was crucified with Christ. His death makes it possible for us to be at peace with God and to experience true righteousness. But the old nature wasn't eradicated, just mortally wounded. It is still alive and at work within you. Your flesh still produces sin in your life. Galatians 5 calls them the "works of the flesh," and lists several areas, like sexual sin, spiritual sin, self-centered sin, and societal sins. As you look through the list you'll see what the flesh produces: adultery, fornication, idolatry, hatred, discord, envy, rage. Those are the expressions of the old man.

When you became a Christian, you didn't lose that old nature. You still have it. Christ comes into your life and gives you a new nature, and the two enter into a holy war. Paul put it this way in Galatians 5:17: "For the flesh lusts against the Spirit, and the Spirit against the flesh; and these are contrary to one another, so that you do not do the things that you wish." A Christian has a much harder time with inner struggles than a non-Christian, because we have these two natures at war within our selves.

This war between old and new natures is the subject of Paul's letter to the Romans. He knows he has been changed, his heart's desire is to follow God, but he finds himself struggling against the flesh. In Romans 7:22 he writes, "I delight in the law of God according to the inward man." That is the normal desire of Christians. There should be a desire within you to love God. There should be a sadness over sin and a wish to please Him. But Paul says, "I see another law in my members, warring against the law of my mind, and bringing me into captivity to the law of sin which is in my members." Even though his heart's desire is to please God, it doesn't automatically happen. There is another force inside—the flesh—that prevents him from pleasing God. He has the desire to do good things, but his performance doesn't measure up. That's why he says, "For the good that I will to do, I do not do; but the evil I will not to do, that I practice."

There is a holy war going on inside every believer. You will face that fight every day, but it doesn't have to be one sad experience after another. There is hope for victory. God has given us a battle plan.

Winning the Inner War

In Galatians 5 we are given two keys to gaining victory over the flesh. One of them is negative and one positive. Notice the 24th verse: "And those who are Christ's have crucified the flesh with it's passions and desires." There is a truth often misunderstood. It is not a positional truth, like the fact that we have been crucified with Christ and had the penalty for our sins paid. It is a description of an action—we have taken the flesh and done something with it.

Crucify the Flesh

While it is a fact that our old nature was positionally crucified when Christ died, it is only true for us as we reckon that truth and apply it in our daily lives. You can believe in your head that Christ crucified the flesh, but if you don't reckon it true and apply it on a daily basis it will never be effective in your life. This is not merely head knowledge; it is the cooperation of your spirit with what happened when Christ died.

The story is told of two men looking at a turtle, still moving though its head was cut off. One of the men examined it and said, "It's dead, but it don't believe it." That's the problem with most Christians. Our old nature died with Christ, but we don't believe it. We keep moving to take it off the cross and use it. We don't recognize that the flesh has been crucified.

John R.W. Stott, in his book on Ephesians, notes three things Christians should understand about crucifixion. First, it was pitiless—an ugly, brutal act used by the Romans on their worst criminals. When Christians crucify the flesh, they need to do so brutally. Second, it was painful—it's never going to feel good when you crucify the flesh. Third, it was permanent—once nailed, a condemned man stayed until he died. Christians must learn not to retract the nails and pull the flesh down so they can indulge in sin again.

Walk in the Spirit

The Holy Spirit is mentioned three times in Galatians 5. Verse 16 says, "Walk in the Spirit." Verse 18 reads, "If you are led by the Spirit." And verse 25 says, "If we live in the Spirit, let us also walk in the Spirit." So you see, we live in the realm of the Spirit. As Christians we understand that He is actively involved in our lives. We are led by the Spirit, who guides and directs us in how we should live. Having nailed the flesh to the cross, you yield to the leadership of the Holy Spirit. You find out where He is leading and you follow Him.

Do you see how you can gain victory over the flesh? You look at those influences in your life that clearly come from the old nature, the ones that are corrupting you and keeping you from having joy in your life. Deal with them ruthlessly, count yourself dead to them, and begin following the guidance of the Holy Spirit. Soon you'll find the fruits of the spirit in verses 22-23 replacing those character traits of the old man. That's what happens to a Christian; God replaces the old character with a new one. Life change for a Christian is not just a matter of stopping things, of tearing out the weeds that have grown in the garden of your life. It is a matter of letting God start some new things by planting seeds to grow a harvest of righteousness. God doesn't tell you to give up something without telling what He is going to replace it with. Romans 13:14 puts it, "But put on the Lord Jesus Christ, and make no provision for the flesh, to fulfill it's lusts."

Don't allow yourself in a situation where the flesh is going to take control. Submit to Christ, and ask God to deal with those areas of your life in opposition to Him. James tells us to "Submit to God, resist the devil, and he will flee from you" (James 4:7). If you spend all your time trying to resist the devil, he's not going to flee. But if, while resisting him, you submit to God, Satan will be defeated. If you spend all your time crucifying the flesh and never yield to the Holy Spirit, you're going to lose the war. But if in the process of crucifying the flesh you are also yielding to the Spirit, you are going to find victory in the war, that holy war that goes on in your life.

APPLICATION

1. According to Galatians 5:16-26, who are the opponents in the Christian's inner holy war?

What does it mean to live in the Spirit?

What are the results of living in the Spirit?

What areas of life does Paul include in the desires of the sinful nature?

As you contrast the acts of the sinful nature with the fruit of the Spirit, what differences do you see?

What do they reveal about the source of each?

2. What do the following verses teach us about the inner battle?

Romans 6:1-2 & 8-14

Romans 7:4-6

Romans 8:1-14

Romans 12:1-2

1 Corinthians 9:24-27

1 Corinthians 10:13

2 Corinthians 5:17

2 Corinthians 7:1

Philippians 3:17-21

Colossians 1:10-14

1 Timothy 6:11-12

3. As you examine your life, where do you feel torn between good and bad desires?

How do you normally deal with it?

Do you know a mature Christian who manifests the fruit of the Spirit? Describe what is unique about his or her life.

How can the insights of this study help you in your struggle with the old nature?

4. How do we crucify our flesh (our old sin nature)?

If we have done that, why must we make a daily decision to "keep in step with the Spirit"?

How does walking in the Spirit guard you from sin?

Is it possible to win the war against the old nature by ourselves? Why not?

5. Read Romans 7:7-25. In your own words, what does Paul say about his struggle?

What does he desire?

Why is it such a struggle?

What does Paul mean when he says, "It is sin living in me"?

How does he resolve his dilemma?

What is the lesson of James 1:12-15?

6. What word best expresses your feelings toward the spiritual battle?

As you look back over this study, what stands out as being most important?

How can you apply what you have studied?

What are you praying for God to do next?

DID YOU KNOW?

Galatians 5:25 reads, "If we live in the Spirit, let us also walk in the Spirit." The word translated "walk" was a military word that Paul appropriated to depict the Christian life. The word literally means "to march in step," and was used by Roman soldiers when they were to march in a parade or a show of force. Paul, who borrowed military terminology throughout Ephesians 6, uses a soldier's term here to convey keeping in step with God's Holy Spirit, being so in tune it is as though you were walking together, side by side. That's the kind of relationship God is calling you into.

OTHER STUDY GUIDES & BOOKS
AVAILABLE THROUGH TURNING POINT

Audio cassette albums are also available. For information use our toll-free number.

SELECTION	CODE	QTY	PRICE	TOTAL
Escape the Coming Night—Messages from Revelation				
Revelation Study Guide, 4 volume package	REVSTP	____	$25.	$ _____
Revelation Study Guide, Volume 1 only	REVSG1	____	$ 8.	_____
Revelation Study Guide, Volume 2 only	REVSG2	____	$ 8.	_____
Revelation Study Guide, Volume 3 only	REVSG3	____	$ 8.	_____
Revelation Study Guide, Volume 4 only	REVSG4	____	$ 8.	_____
Acts of Love: The Power of Encouragement Study Guide	POESG	____	$ 8.	_____
For Such a Time as This—Esther Study Guide	ESTSG	____	$ 8.	_____
Ten Burning Questions from Psalms Study Guide	TBQSG	____	$ 8.	_____
Knowing the God You Worship Study Guide	KGWSG	____	$ 8.	_____
Seeking Wisdom—Finding Gold Study Guide	WISSG	____	$ 8.	_____
Turning Toward Integrity—A Study of James (Book with Study Guide)	TTIBK	____	$10.	_____
Turning Toward Joy—A Study of Philippians (Book with Study Guide)	TTJBK	____	$10.	_____
Turning Toward Freedom—A Study of Galatians (Book with Study Guide available Summer 1995)	TTFBK	____	$10.	_____

BOOKS

The Handwriting on the Wall: Secrets from the Prophecies of Daniel	HOW BK	____	$12.	_____
Escape the Coming Night: The Bright Hope of Revelation	REV BK	____	$10.	_____
Acts of Love: The Power of Encouragement	POE HBK	____	$18.	_____
Invasion of Other Gods—The New Age Spirituality	IOG HBK	____	$18.	_____

For Information and MasterCard, Visa, or Discover Orders Call: **1-800-947-1993** $10 minimum for credit card orders.	**POSTAGE AND HANDLING CHART** For Orders — Add Up to $19.99 — $1.50 $20.00-$50.99 — $3.00 $51.00-$99.99 — $6.00 $100.00 & over — $9.00	MERCHANDISE TOTAL _____ SHIPPING/HANDLING _____ **SUBTOTAL** _____ CA RESIDENTS ONLY ADD 7.25% TAX _____ **TOTAL** $_____

Please enclose payment with order. Make check or money order payable to:

TURNING POINT • P.O. Box 3838 • San Diego, CA 92163-1838 *(Please allow 4-6 weeks for delivery.)*

Mr/Mrs/Miss _____

Address _____

City/State/Zip _____

I listen to *Turning Point* on station: _____

1998 Turning Point Study Guide Project

Dr. Jeremiah and Turning Point deeply appreciate those
who have contributed in financially underwriting
the production of this Study Guide.

The Jerry Jelinek Family

In Memory of Robert Ward

In Honor of Alice Paisley

Bob and Clare Rigel

Ora and Theodore - Flora and Leonard

The Ward Carlson Family

Reimer Senior Care - Visalia

In Memory of Joy Krueger Duncan